It's The Landing That Counts

Finding Peace, Happiness, and Prosperity When Your Life Falls Apart

by

Margot Micallef & Warren Broad

http://www.itsthelandingthatcounts.com

It's The Landing That Counts: How To Find Peace, Happiness & Prosperity When Your Life Falls Apart

Disclaimer & FTC Notice

Dedication

This book is dedicated to my mum and my aunt who fought hardship head on and overcame it; To my dad who quietly showed resilience by going around hardship; To my sister, Gabriella who showed me how grace can diffuse fear and pain; and to my son, Christopher, when you were small your whispered, "I love you" gave me strength to bound over all obstacles and now that you are grown you lift me right over them. I love you all.

-Margot Micallef

To my father who has been there with me through every stage of my life. The man who taught me the power of the written word and perseverance in spite of the odds.

-Warren Broad

Your Free Gifts

As a way of saying thank you for purchasing this book, we're offering our FROM FREEFALL TO FREEDOM 7 day mini-course for FREE, to help you start taking back control of your life immediately. Additionally, we've also included a bonus audio meditation series to help you move towards peace, happiness and prosperity.

These bonuses are valued at over $297 and are our way of saying, "Thank You" for investing in the book and in transforming your life.

To get exclusive access to these bonuses, go to:

http://itsthelandingthatcounts.com

Table Of Contents

Introduction

Mike Tyson said it best.

"Everyone has a plan until they get punched in the face."

If you're reading this book, you've likely been "punched in the face" emotionally, spiritually, or financially. When moments before, life seemed to have a clear and defined plan, now it feels uncertain, terrifying, and upside down. You're in a Free Fall.

You're in a free fall when your life suddenly seems out of control. Maybe you've been unexpectedly fired from your job, or your lover leaves you, or your children disappoint and betray you, or you feel like your life has no purpose, or you're in dire straits financially (maybe you even bought this book with your last few dollars) or maybe you've lost a loved one.

You're likely reeling from the shock and uncertainty of it all. You're probably wondering how things got to this point. Maybe everything you believed in – your entire foundation – feels shaken to the core and you don't know how you're going to move forward.

It can be a very painful place to be. It can feel like you just got punched in the stomach and had all the wind knocked out of you. The hurt just won't seem to go away.

We want you to know that relief is in sight. This book is made just for you. By reading it, you will learn how to turn your life from a place of free fall and uncertainty, into one where, much like a falling cat, you land on your feet, reclaim your life, and move forward, better than ever before. You'll learn how to move into peace, happiness, and prosperity.

By the end of this book, you will realize that it really is the landing that counts. That no matter what life throws at you, you can land on your feet, dust the dirt off, and live a life that exceeds even the best moments you had before the free fall.

Now, you're probably thinking that that's a tall order, and we commend you for being skeptical. But in reading this book, you'll be given the tools to handle life's biggest challenges so you can find that peace, happiness, and prosperity that you're so desperately seeking in your current state of free fall.

But first, we want you to know that we've been through it. We've had the rug pulled out from underneath us; through relationship break ups, death of loved ones, being fired from successful jobs, and deep depression. Yet, through these moments of darkness, despair, and fear, we've found the tools, techniques, and strategies for transforming the worst moments in our lives, into the greatest opportunities to create an even better life for ourselves.

"Every adversity, every failure, every heartache, carries within it the seed of an equal or greater benefit." – Napoleon Hill

And we want you to know this: Even though it hurts like hell right now and though it seems as if there is no light at the end of the tunnel, or that there is no way this pain could possibly heal, we promise you this: you will move through this crisis, and become stronger, happier, and more fulfilled when you come out the other side.

About This Book

This book is an active journey. It's not something you just read passively and then go back to what you were doing in your life. No, this book is meant to be a road map to your recovery. It details the exact process that we used to pull ourselves out of our agonizing free fall, into a life of peace, happiness and prosperity. It will take work - that we can promise - but we'll be here guiding you the whole way, holding your hand and showing you what to do and how to do it. Why go through this effort? Because, what lies on the other side of this journey is peace, happiness, and prosperity.

In this book, we'll start by understanding the free fall itself – what to do when your life is in chaos. This leads us to what we call the Faith Phenomenon, our starting point in this journey to recovery. We'll then identify your internal dialogue and learn how to control the negative self-talk that is sabotaging your recovery, and keeping you from seeing the good that is currently coming your way. And if you don't believe that good is coming, take comfort in this small hope: the fact that you're reading this book means that there is good moving towards you.

After that, you'll learn how to actively use hypnotic meditation to shift your mindset and rapidly put yourself on the road to recovery. No matter what you've heard or done in regards to meditation up to this point, the process we will teach you will impact you more powerfully than any form of meditation can or will in the future.

Next, we'll identify new outcomes for your life and plant the seeds for a newer, brighter future. You'll start to find joy and hope again, looking forward to the things that are coming your way, instead of that debilitating, overwhelming feeling of pain where you want to lay in bed all day and hide from the world.

You'll learn the powerful tool of visualization to rapidly bring your new goals and positive outcomes into your life, and you will start to feel truly excited about the future.

Next, you will learn practical tools to start implementing these changes in your life and take action to move yourself out of your free fall. You'll begin to actively create healing, hope, and new opportunities in your life.

Yes, roadblocks will come up. There will be times when you will want to retreat into yourself, put the blanket over your head, order in Chinese food and block out the world. There will be times when you feel like you're taking a step backward for every two steps you take forward. So we'll teach you how to overcome these roadblocks so you can kick fear in the face, stop the self-sabotage, and live a happy life – no matter what comes your way.

You'll learn how to pick yourself up when you fall again – and you most definitely will fall again (everyone does) – but we'll teach you how to get back up. You will be able to defeat the obstacles with grace and speed.

You'll learn how to keep yourself positive and hopeful, by utilizing the awesome power of *active gratitude* in your life, so you can defend against further setbacks and keep life's challenges in perspective.

After that, you'll be well on your way to claiming your new life and continuing your new journey. You will land and you'll learn to recognize and celebrate the landing. You'll see how much you've moved forward from all the pain, despair, and darkness, even if, right now, it doesn't feel like you'll ever get there.

And finally, you'll cement your new life by giving back, and helping others who are going through a similar situation as you have. You will help others to find peace, happiness and prosperity, as you have done or have started to do.

So, go ahead, take a deep breath. We know it doesn't feel like it, but you will make it through this. Take our hands. Let us show you the road from free fall to peace, happiness and prosperity.

We have purposely formatted wide margins and lots of space between paragraphs to enable you to make lots of notes and treat this book as a workbook for mastering your life.

Chapter 1:

The Free Fall & The Faith Phenomenon

"The thing that we call failure is not falling but staying down."

Mary Pickford

Thoughts From Margot:

I can remember how devastated I was. My life had been completely changed in one single moment. I felt like a rug had been pulled out from underneath me, as I lay emotionally shattered, embarrassed, with everyone I knew to see it.

There was no place to hide. Everything had changed after one conversation.

I was a high level executive, making a great living working for one of the most prestigious companies in Canada. I had worked hard to make it to the top as one of the few women to become a Senior Vice President of the company.

I had given everything to this company, and in a moment, they pulled the rug from under me, firing me without explanation.

"Sorry, Margot. We're going to let you go."

That was it. No concern for the fact that I had given years of my life to this company and that there had been no forewarning.

Minutes before, I was confident and secure. I was comfortable in my future. Now, someone had released the trap door from under me. I was in free fall; my life pulled apart, tumbling into uncertainty, doubt and fear. I started questioning everything that I had known up to that point.

If your own life is in a free fall, we want you to know that we understand. We know how confusing, scary and debilitating free fall is. We know what it's like to doubt everything that you thought was certain. We have felt the overwhelming fear, where you feel like your life has no purpose or meaning. We know what it's like to feel so filled with rage, pain, or sadness that you think there is no way you could ever feel peace again. And even worse than feeling this pain, rage or sadness, is the feeling that you are in this alone, that no one could understand and that no one else has ever experienced these terrible feelings.

First off, we want you to know you are not alone. This feeling that hurts like hell right now, is not unique to you, and that's a good thing. Because it means that, like those who have experienced free fall before you, you too can get through your free fall. You can rise from the ashes of what feels like a shattered life into a new and better one.

Thoughts From Warren:

At age 25, I experienced what would best be called a nervous breakdown. It began with a progressive loss of memory. I went from being essentially fully functional to not being able to remember the most basic of tasks. The deterioration began about 6 months after the passing of my mother.

I felt as though I had been robbed. At such an early age I knew of nobody in my immediate circles that had lost their mother. I was confronted with dealing with yet another situation early in life that nobody else seemed to have to deal with.

I felt completely alone, lost, confused and like I had been given no tools to manage this type of thing. How was I supposed to manage the rest of my life?

I spent about 3 months in deep depression and severe anxiety. I cried daily. I had little short or long-term memory and had to be reminded daily of what my responsibilities were each day.

Eventually I became aware that I could not remain in this state of depression. I had to begin to see a new future for myself. I began to play with new ideas about how I might re-create myself.

In my late 20's I was staring at addiction dead on. I had known for many years I was addicted. I had made attempts to stop before - even going as far as entering treatment.

Again, I felt alone, depressed, and sad. I was confronted with an overbearing massive life change and task that seemed beyond achievement.

One thing that was massively powerful for me in recovery was when I read the "Power of Now" by Eckhart Tolle. Hearing about his struggles within himself brought me to a moment of realization, where I thought, "Holy cow, I'm not alone. I'm not even remotely alone. What I'm going through here, what my mind is having issues with, other people have these issues too."

One of the major problems in free fall, is that we feel so alone. We have the constant thought that, "I'm the only one going through this." There is a feeling of isolation and shame when we think we are so alone in our experience - that no one could possibly connect with our pain. The real power of books like this, is that it lets you know that you are not alone. Knowing that you're not alone in this experience and pain is the first step in healing.

Rest assured, if you are reading this book while you are in a crisis situation, and you implement the teachings in the book, by the time you get to the end you will have, not necessarily landed, because your outcome might not have occurred, but the pain of the crisis will be eased. In this book, you have a road map to get you to where you want to be, where you need to be to land well, and, ultimately, you will be in control of your life again.

The Faith Phenomenon

Humans are incredible beings. Unlike any other known form of life, we are actually capable of projecting into the future an end game that we have in mind for our lives. We are able to consciously choose where we want to be and what we want to accomplish. That's incredible.

Not only is that ability to choose amazing, but we are also capable of cultivating a deep sense of certainty that we will achieve the outcome that we desire. We are capable of having a deep faith that we will achieve what we set out to accomplish, even when we have no clue how it could be possible.

What does this have to do with you?

This brings us to the first stage in moving from free fall to a life of peace, happiness and prosperity. We call it the Faith Phenomenon.

The Faith Phenomenon is the starting point to reclaiming control over your life and is crucial to cultivate if you want to get your life back on track as quickly as possible.

What is the Faith Phenomenon?

The Faith Phenomenon is comprised of two elements. The first is when you have an end goal in mind. It happens when you know precisely what you want to achieve and you are absolutely focused on accomplishing that outcome. The Faith Phenomenon becomes manifested through your "knowing" that the outcome will be as you predicted.

The second element is when you have no idea what is going to happen - or even what needs to happen - but, nonetheless, you have a belief that the outcome will be the right one for you. Let's look closer at these two elements.

The End in Mind - Knowing

Thoughts From Warren

> *When we call on our imagination and higher self to have faith in a new outcome, or new direction, and remain focused and emotionally attached, we will inevitably move towards that envisioned goal or reality.*

Have you ever heard of the expression "begin with the end in mind"? Well, that's exactly the starting point of the Faith Phenomenon. When you have an end in mind, you clearly *know* where you want to go and are wholly committed to manifesting the outcome that you've envisioned.

In the context of the Faith Phenomenon, this "knowing" isn't just positive thinking. We're not talking about just pushing away negative thoughts (although that's important). We don't mean pretending that you have achieved your end goal when you haven't. It's about having a deep sense of *knowing* that the outcome is to be.

Thoughts From Margot:

There is a lot of uncertainty in my line of work. After I started my merchant banking business, called Oliver Capital Partners, I had the opportunity to work with a group of established radio broadcasting operators. Together, we envisioned buying small and mid-sized radio stations throughout Canada and consolidating the operations into a single operating platform and management team. This would save us money by reducing duplicate management and operating costs. It would also allow us to grow revenue by being able to hire and retain more experienced and senior operating and "on air" staff, since we could amortize their costs among a broader platform of stations.

*This idea first sprang up in 2004, but at the time, we had very little money and knew of no radio stations for sale. However, we never doubted we would succeed. We made projections, we were able to obtain a bank loan with a major global bank, and we started to build our company – all this BEFORE we had any radio stations to buy or sufficient money on hand to fulfill our business plan. The key was that we **knew** what we wanted. We **knew** - in the way that you know something deep in your heart with unwavering belief - that we would succeed. And of course we did.*

By February of 2005, we had acquired our first radio station. By September 2005, we had acquired an additional 19 radio stations and by October 2012 we had acquired over 50 radio stations in 3 provinces in Canada.

The first step in using the Faith Phenomenon in your recovery from free fall is to cultivate a deep sense of faith that you *will* create the outcome that you want. You have to believe that the new outcome you want in your life *will come true* - whether that is finally breaking free of addiction, finding meaningful employment again, falling in love again, or recovering from the devastating loss of a loved one. You must begin to cultivate a deep *knowing* that you will – without a doubt – find the peace, happiness or prosperity you are so desperately seeking.

So, how do you do this? How do you cultivate faith? One of the most powerful ways to do this is through visualization. In an upcoming chapter, we'll share with you exactly how to practice visualization to strengthen your belief in your desired outcome. We'll also teach you how to identify your desired outcomes so you know where you want to go from here. This will help you proactively tap into the power of the Faith Phenomenon.

Another way to cultivate this faith is to tie your desired outcome to an act of service for others. When an idea is bigger than you and serves more than just yourself, it has more power. It's easier to believe in and sustain it. So, for example, if you've lost your job, start to become committed to the idea of finding work that not only blesses you but benefits someone else in need as well.

Thoughts From Warren:

> *When I made the leap to starting my private hypnosis practice, my vision held two components. I wanted to be successful with a specific number of clients in mind. I was also deeply connected to helping others and seeing them become successful by finding freedom from their addictions, depression, and life challenges, with my instruction. This desire to help others gave a much deeper conviction to my vision. It gave deeper meaning, strength and purpose to the direction I was going in and dramatically increased my faith in my desired outcome.*

On April 3, 1968, Dr. Martin Luther King, Jr. took to the stage to give what would become his last public speech. Dr. King had been tirelessly working for civil rights, facing an uphill battle the entire way, seeking to change a society that was very much in a state of crisis and free fall. On that night, even though he would never live to see the fruits of his tireless labor to end racism in the United States, he spoke with absolute faith and confidence in the outcome when he spoke these immortal words:

"Like anybody, I would like to live a long life; longevity has its place. But I'm not concerned about that now. I just want to do God's will. And He's allowed me to go up to the mountain. And I've looked over. And I've seen the Promised Land. I may not get there with you. But I want you to know tonight, that we, as a people, will get to the Promised Land. So I'm happy, tonight. I'm not worried about anything. I'm not fearing any man."

– Dr. Martin Luther King, Jr.

Dr. King's faith in the outcome served more than just him, it served others. This allowed him to stay steadfast when most others would have given up, but he had faith in what society could become, despite the extreme crisis of the situation.

Believe In The Outcome Even Though It's Unknown

The second element in the Faith Phenomenon is when you have no idea what is going to happen or even what you want or need to have happen. In these moments where life seems unclear and uncertain, you can invoke the Faith Phenomenon by believing that the outcome will be what it needs to be, and that it will be the right one for you.

Thoughts From Warren:

> *When I was coming out of my breakdown I knew I had to begin moving back into society and life. Taking a job as a laborer with a stonemason was not glamorous in any way. But I had to have faith. I had to have faith that taking action and challenging myself and my mind's dialogue would bear fruit. I had to have faith that my life would get better, even if I didn't know how.*

Maybe you have recently separated from your spouse. It's easy to feel alone and vulnerable, and have no idea what you want. You're likely longing for the fulfillment of the dream of your life together. When you want something, yet it is not within your grasp or control, you may feel sick to your stomach with fear. It's at this time when it's most important to have faith that things will get better and turn out right for you. There is truth in the old saying, "This too shall pass."

Thoughts From Margot:

> *Shortly after my marriage[1] ended, I went to see a massage therapist. After the treatment, she gave me a small, shiny stone with the word "faith" engraved on it. It reminded me that the Faith Phenomenon was on my side. I carried that stone with me for months. Whenever I wondered what my next step was to be, where or with whom I might end up, or when the pain would stop, I touched that stone and repeated the words, "Faith in the outcome."*

> *This faith did not instantly clarify for me what I was supposed to do in that moment or what was going to happen, but it did bring tremendous relief in the form of that deep sense of knowing that the outcome would be right for me.*

Faith has to precede all action. Even though you may feel like your life couldn't possibly recover from the devastating crisis that you're in – that you'll never love again, never find work, never trust again, or always be an addict – you have to believe

---

[1] My reference to "marriage" in this book is NOT a reference to any one relationship, but rather is a composite of a number of relationships – platonic or intimate – that I shared with people who were once in my life but are no more. This is done to protect the privacy of these relationships while still enabling me to share with our readers the pain flowing from the end of such relationships and the strength in moving on from them. MMM

that your life can and will get better, and that you can create the vision of your life that you've always wanted.

The Faith Phenomenon is on your side and will bring you to a safe landing on your feet. Take a deep breath and start to believe in it. Let the words "faith in the outcome" be your mantra.

Our next step in getting through this free fall is to break the constant negative internal dialogue which sabotages your success.

Chapter 2:

Break That Broken Record - Recognizing & Stopping The Internal Dialogue

From Margot:

My dad lost his job when I was fifteen. He was never able to find another job again. He was a university professor who spoke nine languages. He had five degrees, and was absolutely brilliant. Yet, despite all of his education, he wasn't able to find another job.

I remember one day, even though I was moving on after being fired, I suddenly had this little voice inside me that started questioning my optimism. It shrieked at me, "Who do you think you are? Some people never recover from being fired. Why do you think you can?" These words really set me back and completely shook my confidence.

That sinister voice inside my head popped up and assaulted me in the midst of my progress and efforts at moving out of my free fall.

You know the voice that we're talking about. It's that obnoxious broken record that plays over and over and over again in your head, telling you all the reasons why you won't succeed. It tells you that you're an imposter and that things will continue to get worse.

It's the voice that says:

"I'll never find a job."

"I'll always be alone."

"Happiness is a myth."

"I'll always be broke."

"I'm not good enough..."

You know the drill. It's a broken record we like to call your negative self-talk or NST.

NST emanates from your mind. It is that little voice or those constant thoughts inside your head that tear you down, weaken your resolve and destroy your self-esteem and confidence. NST is often based on ideas, circumstances, and responses that we've had to different events in our lives.

It could be friends playfully teasing in the playground, a teacher who thought she was inspiring us as children, or a coach who thought he was toughening us up. It's almost always about the way **WE** perceived how others felt about us. NST is typically a *self-directed* type of criticism, based on how we perceive an experience.

Frankly, few messages that others say to us are maliciously intended (although some absolutely are). Most of us developed this NST from the unintended perception of the most well intentioned messages. It could have been meant as an optimistic perspective, a voice of encouragement, or even a sense of pride. But we interpreted it as pressure, as an expectation, as a judgment of our ability, character or performance.

Many parents express displeasure with their kids by withdrawing the visible expression of love as a means of disciplining or controlling their children. This *can* (and we stress *can* not *will*) lead to a child perceiving that they are "not good enough". Every parent unintentionally leaves their child with some sort of baggage that we have to overcome as adults. Often that baggage relates to our own perception of ourselves.

If you were told as a child that you were not going to achieve anything grand, because you lacked discipline, or weren't smart enough, or had some other limitation, then you likely ended up with a very strong negative self-talk of, "I'm never going to succeed." And if you do succeed despite this belief system, it will often haunt you at the most inopportune time to tell you that you are a fraud and don't deserve to succeed. Again, notice how NST directs the criticism at ourselves based on how we interpret an experience.

Sometimes people succeed despite their NST. Sarah McLachlin, an international music star, winner of many Grammy and Juno awards, and successful by any standard, recently confessed that she harbors "deep self-doubt". This secret self-loathing is not uncommon.

Even though you have succeeded, if you don't stop the NST, you may undermine your success and fail after the fact. Why do you think there are so many "rags to riches to rags" stories? Many of the real life heroes in these stories used their NST to reach success (i.e. it drove them to work hard to prove themselves) but once they reached the pinnacle their NST tore apart their success, brick by brick.

Occasionally there is no direct event or person that triggers this negative self-talk. Sometimes it just exists for reasons that might not be obvious to us.

Our NST will "protect" us from this discomfort by steering us towards the things that make us comfortable. So instead of asking someone out on a date we engage in activities that we are comfortable doing alone; instead of allowing ourselves to risk rejection or be vulnerable in an intimate relationship we hold back, close up and refuse to open up in a relationship; instead of asking for a raise or starting a new venture we stay in a dead end, underpaying job; instead of joining a gym or going to a yoga class we make up excuses about why we can't work out. In the end, refusing to get out of our comfort zone prevents us from living life to the fullest and realizing our deepest desires.

Negative self-talk can also come from trauma. Maybe you were abused, assaulted or experienced some other traumatic experience in your life. Or maybe it wasn't physical trauma but emotional trauma, like being laughed at when you had to read a chapter out of an English book in front of the class or you struggled with a math problem when the teacher called on you to answer a question.

Regardless of how our perception of ourselves was formed, most of us have experienced NST in some form.

Words to watch out for

Be careful how you speak to yourself. Some words you may say to yourself are downright nasty. They can destroy your efforts to succeed and suck the life out of you, leaving you feeling crippled in your path to recovery.

The message you often convey with NST is "I'm not good enough" (or some variation of it). Whether that message relates to your job, your love life, your family or friends, it's easy to blame yourself for the circumstance you find yourself in.

Here are some other variations to watch out for:

I'm not smart enough.

I'm not sexy enough.

I'm not funny enough.

I'm not compassionate enough.

I'm not open enough.

I'm not pretty enough.

I'm not skinny enough.

I'm not engaging enough.

I'm not patient enough.

I'm not strong enough.

I'm not funny enough.

I'm not entertaining enough.

I'm not _____(fill in the blank) enough.

Have you ever said any of these messages to yourself?

When we attribute our crises to our insufficiency around the belief that we're not good enough we *prolong* our free fall. It devalues who we are, chains us to our past, and prevents us from changing what we do, because, after all, with NST it wasn't what we did that caused our crisis, but *who we are.*

In other words, the most challenging part about negative statements like these is that they are absolute. There is no degree of variability in them. They paint a broad brush stroke across the canvas of our emotions and essentially say, "This is just how it is." It's pretty hard to argue with something when it feels like it's absolute.

This is why it's so important to stop and talk to yourself in a different way.

Talk To Yourself Like You Would Talk To A Loved One

Here's a question. If a close friend, family member, or a young child had just gone through a traumatic experience, would you ever say to them, "Well, it's because you're not good enough."

NO!

You know that the message would only make things worse and be emotionally damaging to them. What's crazy is we have no problem doing this to ourselves – and we're all guilty of it.

In Guy Winch's great book *Emotional First Aid*[2], he talks about how when we fall and break a bone, we give ourselves time to recover. We perform or accept first aid and give ourselves the medical treatment necessary. We stay in bed. We nurture our broken leg. We rest and recover. We *do not* go run a marathon right away. And we certainly don't intentionally smack our broken bone against the wall.

However, when it comes to our emotions when we're in free fall, this is *exactly* what we do. We replay the event over and over in our mind. We use if/then statements such as, "*If* I was smarter and worked harder *then* I wouldn't have been fired." "*If* I had lost 10 pounds *then* he wouldn't have left me." "*If* I would have done this or that differently, *then* everything would be different." What we're basically doing with these if/then statements is smashing our broken emotional bones against a

[2] Guy Winch, Emotional First Aid, Hudson Street Press, New York, NY 2013

31

wall, over and over again, reliving the pain, and making our situation and the prospect of recovery worse.

We would never do that to our body. We would never do that to someone we loved. Yet, we do that with our emotions.

Instead of saying "if/then" and making the problem worse, what if you talked to yourself like you were talking to your 10-year-old niece or nephew?

What if you said things like, "Hey, I know today was really hard for you. It probably seemed like nothing was going right. But, you've been through really challenging things before and made it out the other side. This is going to be no different. You've got my love and support 100%, and if you just need a shoulder to cry on, that's okay, because I'll always be here for you, and you're a strong person. I believe in you. I love you and I'll be here for you. We can make it through this."

Thoughts From Margot:

> *When I was in free fall after my husband[3] and I split up I would beat myself up and blame myself for what happened. I kept wishing I had done things differently. I kept playing our last conversation in my mind and saying to myself, "Why didn't I insist we talk through our*

---

[3] The reference to "my husband" as used in this book is NOT a reference to any one person, but rather is a composite of people (friends and lovers) with whom I have shared love and lost love. This is done to protect the privacy of these people while still enabling me to share with our readers the pain of lost love and the joy of recovering from it. MMM

problems? Why did I just agree it was over? Why didn't I fight back and tell him I didn't want to split up?"

Then one day, after I had shed many tears, I had a vision of myself as a five-year-old child. And I closed my eyes and picked myself up and sat my five year old self on my adult lap and cuddled myself and told myself I was ok. I consoled myself by taking care of that broken, sad part of me that resembled a small child in need of love.

Trouble Changing The Internal Conversation?

What if you're having a really hard time talking to yourself in this kinder, gentler way? What if you're having a challenging day where you can't seem to stop the negative emotional clamor in your mind?

If you don't have it within yourself to know how to talk to yourself with love or you can't think of anything good to say about yourself, ask a friend. Ask them to tell you how wonderful you are. Ask them to tell you what they like about you and what makes you different than everyone else.

And if you can't find a friend to tell you how wonderful you are, identify somebody else out there, an actor, a teacher, a colleague, or somebody you admire, and identify what their strong points are. Internalize those qualities and act as if you possess those strong points. It's usually easier to find the good in other people and then proactively work to claim it as our own.

This technique is extrapolated from the research of Dr. Amy Cuddy, Associate Professor at Harvard Business School. Dr. Cuddy showed that if a person took on (or "faked") the body postures which are associated with dominance and power (for a minimum of two minutes at a time) even if they didn't feel dominant or confident in advance of taking on these body positions, they tended to act more powerfully, feel more confident and perform better. So, while Dr. Cuddy's research relates to a different behavior, namely non-verbal expressions, we see parallels between our recommendation and her research and her recent summary of her research, namely: "fake it until you become it".

And just in case you truly have no one in your life to tell you anything wonderful about you, we want you to personally know that we think you are amazing. Out of all the people in the world in free fall, you have the courage to read a book like this and begin the journey to reclaiming your life. That means you are a courageous person, and we're honored to share this journey with you.

Is That A Monkey In My Mind?

Not all negative talk is destructive. Some negative conversations we have with ourselves are necessary in helping us identify inappropriate behavior. It is possible that the negative voices you are hearing actually have a useful purpose. But how do we distinguish between the useful messages and the destructive ones?

In eastern philosophy, there is a term that is sometimes used to describe the clamoring voices in our heads. It's called "Monkey Mind". It comes from Hindu philosophy and is that part of our mind that never wants to sit still or focus on long-term goals.

Monkey Mind is circular. It's why when you start down the path of telling yourself things like, "I'm not good enough", that it can start to spiral and feel as if you are mindlessly spinning around and around – like you've been caught in a hamster wheel.

Monkey Mind comes from the part of our mind that can't sit still and loves to jump from place to place. It takes the negative self-talk and then worsens and amplifies it until you're spiraling downwards out of control. By getting stuck in this circular pattern – you prevent yourself from being able to break out of your free fall.

We also refer to this process as "snowballing". When you roll a snowball down a mountainside, it grabs more snow, becoming larger and larger until it's almost out of control. This "snowballing" can happen when we're anxious or depressed. At first you may have simply started with a little thought the size of a small snowball in your hand. That might be something like feeling a little short of breath. If allowed to snowball, to let your mind run wild, that may end up turning into a panic attack that is now feeling like a full blown heart attack. Warren has created a video to help you handle this snowballing process. You can access it here:

https://www.youtube.com/watch?v=EmQ5zIYCuqs

Monkey Mind is also immature. It's not a voice of wisdom. It isn't going to provide you with much insight on how to better your situation. Monkey Mind is like a child who will continue to cry until you distract, interrupt, or comfort it.

So how do you know if your internal conversation is coming from a voice of reason that you should listen to? Here's an easy litmus test. Ask yourself these two questions:

Am I feeling any better about my current situation and my future life after listening to my assessment of my situation?

Is what I am being told actually true or factual?

If the answer is "No" then Monkey Mind is taking that NST and dominating the conversation. Good news, it's time to change the conversation.

If the answer is "Yes", then you're listening to the real you, even if that "real you" may be speaking sternly to you. If you've done something that does not align with your values and you scold yourself for doing so, that is not Monkey Mind. It is that voice of wisdom, maturity, and guidance that is the better part of you.

For example: if you stayed out late with your friends, drank too much and flirted with the good looking server while your spouse was at home looking after the kids, you might be unhappy with your behavior. Your stern self might scold you for your inappropriate conduct - and rightly so! The difference is that your stern self is criticizing your behavior and encouraging you to improve it. If Monkey Mind took over the conversation it would become circular and be directed at yourself not at your behaviour. At the end, if your stern self-scolds you and counsels you on how you should behave next time you are the better for it. There may be other times when your stern self, kicks in to correct your behavior and your conversation with yourself would sound something like this:

"I was off my game in that meeting because I got there late. Tomorrow I'll make sure I'm on time."

"I don't feel good being at receptions or networking when I don't know anyone at the event. Next time, I'm going to attend with a colleague."

"I feel terrible speaking in public. I'm going to join Toastmasters."

This constructive conversation should make you feel better about the situation you are unhappy about. Monkey Mind on the other hand would make you feel worse.

Take a moment to remember the conversation that you're having that is making you feel better or relieving your angst. When the negative voices pop up again (and you can be sure they will), then you know how to change the conversation, by directing it at your behavior not at yourself. You can go back to this same productive conversation and start to feel empowered and in control.

Another way to change the conversation and get control of Monkey Mind is to replace it with internal dialogue that is positive. Whenever you start down this circular path, picture in your mind a stop sign – we literally mean a stop sign, the bright red octagonal sign that you see on a street corner – that says **STOP!** See the sign, or better yet, take a photo of it with your phone and open it up when Monkey Mind takes over. Shout the words in your mind (or if no one is around, go ahead and shout it out loud). This active interruption will startle Monkey Mind long enough for you to consciously change the dialogue to something positive.

Once you've interrupted Monkey Mind, look around and find positive things to say to yourself. You might say:

"Wow, what a great day."

"I'm feeling good right this second."

"I'm so blessed to be alive."

"I've got so many other good things going for me right now."

The positive statements can be really simple if you can't muster the energy to say any of the above. Look to find tiny things to feel good about. Things like:

"I am so enjoying this cup of tea"

"The barista down the street has a nice smile"

"The cool air feels so good on my face"

"I'm glad I wore mittens today"

"I love the sun shine"

Thoughts from Margot:

> My sister had the best sense of humor of anyone I knew. She loved to laugh and that did not change when she became ill. She had a small stuffed dog that had a motion detector on it and when someone walked by it, it would roll around and laugh. She named that dog "Pierre" and purposely when she needed to hear a laugh she would walk by Pierre and his laughter and antics would make her smile. After she passed away, I inherited Pierre. For the longest time Pierre sat on my bookshelf, not moving and not laughing. After my husband and I split up, I recall moping around missing him when I spotted Pierre. I flipped the switch to "on" and put Pierre on the floor. He immediately started to roll around and laugh. His laugh was contagious. I now keep Pierre on the floor in my home and, like my sister, when I just need a giggle, I will walk by Pierre and smile as he rolls around and laughs.

Find something to remind you to laugh. It may be a funny cartoon, a YouTube video or a funny memory. Or watch "Pierre" at: **http://youtu.be/TkXeYWn4xaY**

The most important thing is to take control of Monkey Mind and change the conversation.

Take a minute to write down the positive phrases that you say to yourself or others that make you feel good. Keep these in your pocket so you can always be reminded of them. This way, you can go back to this same productive conversation when you need to feel empowered and in control again.

Personalizing

One of the most challenging things about being in a free fall is that people react differently to you after your crisis. Their treatment of you can impact the intensity of the free fall and your recovery from it.

Thoughts From Margot:

> *I remember after I got fired that many people stopped calling me or wouldn't take my calls. These were people who I had helped along in their career, or who benefitted from the position I held before I got fired. I considered them friends in many cases. The same thing happened when my husband and I broke up. It seemed that some people immediately thought about themselves and felt that in order to gain the best advantage from my crisis, or to preserve or protect their position, they needed to take sides. In some cases the side they chose was not mine. I found that disconnection excruciatingly painful and it intensified the feeling of isolation and fear.*

When we are in a free fall it's common to interpret other people's behavior as a judgment of ourselves. It is easy to take other people's behavior personally. But you shouldn't.

The reality is that other people are impacted by our circumstances, but they are interpreting the same set of circumstances from their own perspective. Their behavior is not a reflection of you. It is a reflection of them.

They may be afraid of how your departure from your job might impact their role with your former employer. Or they may feel a sense of loyalty to your former employer or your ex-husband or ex-wife for reasons unknown to you. Irrespective of what is motivating them it is *never* about you. But *always* about them and about what they feel they need to do to protect themselves.

Having said that, it is still painful when we feel the rejection of people we thought were friends. Reminding ourselves that it is about what they feel they need to do to protect themselves, helps us understand and forgive their conduct and overcome the pain of rejection or disconnection.

A Sobering Truth

At the end, here's what matters: getting control of the negative self-talk in your head is one of the most important things you can do. Whether that is NST about a specific belief, activity, or action, or a mind full of constant clamor and restlessness, or interpreting other people's behavior, you must take charge of what is going on in your head. If Monkey Mind is always replaying the pain of the experience that you went through, if you constantly fear what might come from it in the future (financial ruin, embarrassment, you'll be alone for life); if you take other people's behavior personally as a criticism of you, then all you will get is more depression, more pain, more sadness. You will go deeper down the rabbit hole. You'll struggle to end your free fall and land in a place of opportunity.

But we want you to know there is good news. NST does not need to dominate you. You can control the Monkey Mind from spiraling out of control and making you sick with worry or shame. You can learn not to let other people's behavior impact you. And in the next chapter we're going to show you exactly how to begin taking control of your mind and move it from a place of pain to a place of possibility.

Chapter 3:

Shifting Gears – Active Meditation

Once you've identified negative self-talk, the next step in the process is to shift your mindset from a place of suffering to a place of hope and opportunity. The hard part can be figuring out how to do this.

Shifting your mindset is a rational process. It's a conscious choice to decide what to think, instead of letting your mind run wild like a bunch of monkeys. It's about saying, "Hey, is this really the best thing for me to be thinking right now? I'm feeling pretty lousy with this mental conversation running on repeat. How about letting myself be positive and feel better?"

Sometimes a song comes on the radio and all it does is remind you of that ex-lover that broke your heart. All of a sudden you're reliving the end of the relationship and all the feelings that went along with it.

But, if you turn off the music or change the song to one that's upbeat, happy and has no association with the heartbreak, you start to feel better; the mental and emotional flashback eases. You start to enjoy life again.

That's the same thing that we're doing when we shift our mindset. In effect, we're changing the mental radio station so we have different thoughts and feelings.

In the words of Kristen Jongen:

> *"It occurred to me that this reprieve of sadness is a choice. It's a choice to mentally let go of the obsession to worry even in the midst of the storm... The shoe can drop whether or not I am happy, sad, pensive, obsessive, staring at it or enjoying myself. Watching it drop is, in the end, no less painful than hearing it drop and turning to look. Or hearing later that it has dropped. The fallout is the same. ... Why not choose happiness?"4*

In our program *It's The Landing That Counts Master Class*, we show you a powerful process for changing your mindset. Just visit **www.itsthelandingthatcounts.com/masterclass**

Hypnotic Meditation – A Fresh Approach To Meditation

Hypnotic meditation is the key to taking control of your mental imagery and messaging. It's the answer to getting control of Monkey Mind.

---

4 Kristen Jongen, Growing Wings, Soul Soup Publishing LLC, Traverse City, MI 2006 (p. 52/53)

If you are not familiar with hypnosis or meditation, you may be feeling skeptical about trying this technique. You may feel that meditation has a mystical, mysterious aura about it or that it has its roots in the hippy culture of the sixties. You might think that hypnosis is something that entertainers do to make people look silly and lose self-control. So, the thought of combining these two practices may not be very appealing to you.

Let's break each of these practices down a little for you. In some respects we could say that we all meditate without realizing it. When we have those moments of spiritual connectedness, (religious or not) we're meditating. We all have those moments when time seems to drift away; when our mind becomes softer, less rigid and we are not consumed by the monkey clamoring around inside.

Meditation is the letting go of attachments. Letting go of all those things our mind wants to stay so focused on – pain, fear, doubt, anger, and shame. All those things, that in the big picture, often means so little

In meditation we work on being at peace with what is.

Thoughts from Warren:

> *I often ask my clients these questions when they are in a free fall or deep attachment. I ask, "What if you were to simply allow yourself to not care about this issue for 20 minutes?"*

45

The answer, if they are truthful, is generally something like, "Well, I would be happier, less stressed" and so on.
I then ask them, "Why not more than 20 minutes if all these good things could come from releasing the attachment?"

This is what meditation allows. It allows us to disengage for a period of time. And with that disengagement we become free of the monkey and the attachments it wants to play with.

Hypnosis is a state of relaxation during which we are highly focused and susceptible to the power of suggestion. Hypnotic meditation is the combination of meditation techniques coupled with the power of hypnotic suggestion to enable us to reprogram our mind. Once this happens, the mind moves inward, and slows down, instead of buzzing around focusing on all of the external factors.

Think of it as turning off the electricity in your house so you can fix the wiring. Hypnotic Meditation allows you to move into a relaxed state, turn off Monkey Mind and re-program your internal dialogue.

Once we reach that comfortable state, things like visualization and thinking about new possibilities becomes easier, since Monkey Mind cannot live in the hypnotic meditative state. It might try and intrude, but its strength and power is significantly diminished. This hypnotic meditative process lets you focus on healing your life and creating new and exciting possibilities for the future.

So let's walk through how hypnotic meditation works. And if you'd like to actually experience a guided hypnotic meditation, you can access it right here:

http://itsthelandingthatcounts.com/meditation

On Meditation

"Meditation more than anything in my life was the biggest ingredient of whatever success I've had."

-Ray Dalio, Billionaire founder of Bridgewater Associates, the world's largest hedge fund firm, 2012

Thoughts From Warren:

I first heard about meditation while I was trying to overcome my depression. When I was in University, I studied world religions. I'd known that meditation was used by many faiths, so I started looking at different ways that it could help me change my mindset, which was a mess at the time. I knew that in order to move out of this terrifying free fall my life was in - if I was to keep from being engulfed by it - that I'd need some sort of daily process to get me out of it.

As I began to practice daily meditation, something funny happened. It actually worked! I started to heal and become more optimistic about my future. I found a job working in a group home for displaced children, which ultimately led me to the realization of what I wanted to do with my life.

I went back to school and began to study adult psychology, which eventually led me to studying clinical hypnosis. I started to see the power of hypnosis in speeding up the healing process for people who had gone through traumatic free falls in their lives. I also saw, in my life and in hundreds of other lives, how hypnosis could bring us into a state of empowerment. This eventually led us to developing Hypnotic Meditation.

How Hypnotic Meditation Works

So, let's look at how and why hypnotic meditation works so well in speeding up the recovery process in your life.

Activity in our brain is expressed by electrical impulses. These impulses, which are measured by an electroencephalogram (EEG), are referred to as "brainwaves" because of the *"wave-like"* pattern depicted by the EEG when measuring this activity. The frequency or activity level of these brainwaves changes based on the degree of consciousness or wakefulness.

At our most awake state, the brainwaves are tight and short. These brainwaves are known as *Beta* waves and they range in frequency from 13 to 60 pulses per second. In this "Beta state," we are consciously alert. The frequency of the brainwave activity increases along this range as we feel agitated, fearful or tense. We spend most of our day in this state.

As we move from this heightened state of consciousness to a more relaxed state, our brain waves slow down to about 7 to 13 pulses per second. This more relaxed state is called *Alpha*. When we're calm, relaxed and tranquil, this is often the state we're in.

When we fall asleep our brainwave activity drops to about 4 to 7 pulses per second. This state of brain activity is called *Theta*. At this level of brain activity we have some consciousness. When we become unconscious we release 0.1 to 4 pulses per second. This level of brain activity is called *Delta*.

The *Siriaj Medical Journal* diagramed the brain waves in the following ways:

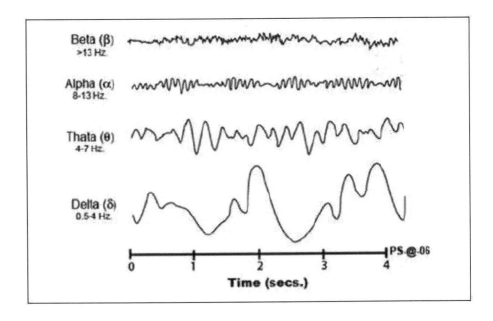

Beta (14-30 Hz)

Concentration, arousal, alertness, cognition

Higher levels associated with Anxiety, disease, feelings of separation, fight or flight

Alpha (8 - 13.9 Hz)

Relaxation, superlearning, relaxed focus, light trance, increased serotonin production

Pre-sleep, pre-waking drowsiness, meditation, beginning of access to unconscious mind

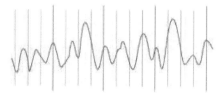

Theta (4-7.9 Hz)

Dreaming sleep (REM sleep)
Increased production of catecholamines (vital for learning and memory), increased creativity

Integrative, emotional experiences, potential change in behavior, increased retention of learned material

Hypnagogic imagery, trance, deep meditation, access to unconscious mind

Delta (0.1-3.9 Hz)

Dreamless sleep
Human growth hormone released

Deep, trance-like, non-physical state, loss of body awareness

Access to unconscious and "collective unconscious" mind,

In general, we live the bulk of our life in a Beta state or a heightened sense of awareness.

When we diminish the brain activity to Alpha, we create the perfect condition to learn new information. In this Alpha state, we produce significant increases in the levels of beta-endorphin, norepinephrine and dopamine, which are mood enhancers and have been linked to feelings of increased mental clarity and memory. This effect lasts for hours and even days.

When we first start to meditate - when we are in a light hypnotic state - we are in an Alpha state. As we increase our proficiency with meditation and hypnosis, we move into the Theta state. There are certain monks who have been studying meditation for years, who may come very close to the Delta state.

The primary goal of meditation is a quiet mind and observation. Hypnosis, on the other hand, is goal-oriented and active. During hypnosis, we visualize and direct our visualization to goals. Therefore, *hypnotic meditation* is a combination of a quiet mind that is open to positive visualization and goal setting. When the practice of meditation is combined with hypnosis, profound results can be achieved.

The key to practicing hypnotic meditation is to intentionally enter into a trance state during the meditation. In a trance state, we are relaxed and highly sensitive to new information.

Can you remember a time in your life when you, or someone you know, was in a trance?

Maybe you were doing something repetitive, such as driving home or taking the subway home from work. You might have made that trip hundreds, if not thousands, of times. You may have experienced getting in the car, and all of a sudden, finding yourself at home. You may not recall the stop signs, the red lights, the left and right hand turns, the busy intersection with the pretty flashing lights or the dark corner immediately before your last turn.

Likewise, you may have experienced getting on the subway and missing your stop. You may not have heard the announcement or noticed the people getting on and off the train. And then all of a sudden, you are "coming to" and wondering, "Where am I?" or, "How did I get here"? If you have ever had an experience like either of these, then you have experienced the trance state.

Two Sides To The Brain

There are two sides to the brain, namely, the left logical, intellectual or active side, and the right creative, intuitive or emotional side. Our left logical side of the brain enters the trance state because we have performed that particular repetitive task of getting home from work so many times that our logical side of the brain goes on "autopilot" and temporarily shuts off. On autopilot, the creative, intuitive side of our brain is able to wander and drift.

We also have two levels of consciousness. The subconscious brain, which heavily impacts and relates to our right creative, intuitive or emotional side, and the conscious brain, which more heavily impacts and relates to our left logical, intellectual or active side.

What does that all mean?

Well, contained within the logical left side of our brain is what we call our "critical mind." The critical mind is the part of our mind that is very attached to our safety. If you are walking through the forest and a tree starts falling toward you, it is the critical mind that thankfully alerts you to get out of the way. The critical mind never completely shuts off. Even when we are in our deepest sleep, it is the critical mind that hears those bumps in the night, or awakens us to a room filling up with smoke. That's the good news.

On the flip side, just as the critical mind can prevent us from remaining in a burning house, it can also prevent us from taking positive steps that it *perceives* might harm us, or it's unfamiliar with. The keyword here is *perceives*. The critical mind likes the status quo. It likes what it's comfortable with and wants to keep things that way. Even though the critical mind doesn't leave us, we can shut it off by letting it believe we are in a safe and comfortable environment. Hypnosis allows us to do that.

When you're in free fall, your critical mind is trying desperately to keep you safe – which is great. However, in order to activate the Faith Phenomenon, it's important to silence the critical mind so you can see what is new and possible for your life.

In hypnosis, you enter into a deeper trance than the trance like state of unconsciously returning home from work. A light trance can be achieved as we move from the waking Beta state to the less aware Alpha state where we stay when we meditate. But as we move into a deep trance, our brain activity slows down even further and we move into the early stage of Theta to achieve a hypnotic state. It is this deep, or Theta trance state, that we refer when we refer to hypnotic meditation.

Because we are in a deep trance in hypnotic meditation, we are able to enter the subconscious mind to reprogram it. In a state of meditation or contemplation short of this deep trance state, the active left side of our brain where the critical mind resides, blocks out any attempts to influence the passive right side where the seat of the subconscious lives.

The right side of the brain is where we can reprogram our minds, visualize what we aspire to, and manifest it into reality. In short, it is where we change our thinking to enable us to soften the landing when we are in a free fall. You will need to disengage your critical mind and allow your subconscious to reprogram your right side of the brain to effectively master the tools and techniques we have laid out for you in the following chapters.

Hypnotic Meditation is the key to unlocking the grip that the critical mind has on your ability to move to that place to which you aspire: peace, happiness and prosperity.

How to Practice Hypnotic Meditation

Now that you know the brain state that you need to enter into, let's look at how to practice hypnotic meditation.

The first step is to enter into a deep trance state. In order to enter into this state you need to create an environment that allows the critical mind to feel at ease. By using a process called progressive relaxation we lull the "critical mind" into a state of relaxation. By following a process of consciously breathing and working through the body systematically, we trick the critical mind into stepping aside.

You cannot rush this process. You must be methodical and allow the body to become relaxed.

One of our favorite methods in creating the hypnotic meditative state is the "heavy body" technique. Let's look at how to do this.

The Heavy Body Meditation Technique

The "heavy body" meditation technique starts with breathing. Start by paying attention to each breath in and each breath out. You can do this by what's called "belly breathing", which is paying attention to the rise and fall of your stomach as you breathe. Because your mind can't be in two places at the same time, what that really forces the mind to do is focus. When you're concentrated on that rise and fall caused by your breathing, you can't be thinking about your surroundings. You can't be thinking about "poor me" and your circumstances. You can't be thinking about anything, because you have to focus on this rise and fall of your breathing. So, stage one is conscious breathing.

Stage two is progressive relaxation. Here you move into "heavy body". The next step is to work from top to bottom, focusing on the different areas of your body. Begin with your scalp, your eyelids, your ears, your mouth, your jaw, your neck, and move right down through the entire body. As you work through each body part you want to relax and release any tension that may exist there.

Go slowly as it is not always easy to bring yourself to a state of relaxation. If you've been able to achieve "heavy body", your body will become so heavy that you will feel as if you cannot lift your arms or legs. Of course you can, if you switch your attention enough to re-animate your arms or legs to move, but if you do so, you will move out of the meditative state. So simply be aware of the sensation without pushing the limit of it.

Now that you've reached "heavy body", you can do a slow countdown from ten down to one in your mind, taking yourself even deeper into relaxation.

At this point you should be deeply relaxed and comfortable. In this state, you're open to what you want to achieve most. So if you're having a really depressed day, the objective during that meditation session might be happiness. You might want to focus on gratitude, or something uplifting that is going to allow you to move out of that depressive funk.

Prayer

You can also move into this trance state through prayer. Since the beginning of time, prayer has been used to create altered states of consciousness. Any ritual, ceremony, action or prayer that is done in a repetitive manner will eventually create a meditative state.

In Catholicism, repeating the rosary is a meditative act in the same way that Gregorian chants are meditative. Muslims who pray multiple times per day in most instances are repeating a single prayer over and over again. If you look at Hasidic Jews at the Wailing Wall in Jerusalem closely, you will have no doubt that you are viewing someone in a deep hypnotic and meditative state.

Most religions understand that the meditative state is a powerful mechanism for deepening our connection to ourselves, God, and our purpose.

Thoughts From Margot:

> *I had heard a lot about meditation, but knew little about it. During my free fall, I would often say that my greatest fear was experienced when I laid down to sleep and when I awoke each morning. I would try and fill my mind with positive thoughts and push away the fear of being in free fall – the loss of my marriage or the loss of my job. In those moments of fear and desperation, I started to pray, endlessly repeating the prayers I had learned as a child growing up in an Italian-Catholic household. The repetition of my prayers helped me disconnect from the negative thoughts filling my mind and brought me a sense of peace. I found that as I slowed down my prayers, they became a sort of mantra that moved me into a deeper awareness and helped me take control of my thoughts. I realized this was a form of meditation for me.*

Achieving The Hypnotic Meditative State

As you enter into your hypnotic meditative state, you will begin to have a subtle awareness of having gone inward. Your focus should no longer be on the external. Your mind is now far more internal and meditative. Now that you've achieved this deeply relaxed state, you are capable of directing your thoughts to a place of your choosing.

Having said that, it is essential to understand that you are not attempting directly to get an answer to a problem or directly aiming to resolve an issue. That activity is too critically and analytically minded. If you move to this state of active thinking, you will move out of your trance and lose the meditative hypnotic state.

In this hypnotic meditative state, you can move to a state of mind that is openly positive. The mind loves positive imagery and will gladly accept visualizations, images and thoughts that depict outcomes that are positive and affirming. In an upcoming chapter, we'll show you how to pair visualization with hypnotic meditation to get the most out of it.

In this positive state you can begin to manage your free fall, preparing for the landing you aspire to. This is where you actively amplify the Faith Phenomenon in your life. When you move to a place in your mind that allows you to create and visualize your desired outcome, you've gone from a place of being passive in your life to a place of activity and movement. And, remember, it is movement that causes change in our life. You can't get out of a crisis by staying where you are.

This movement opens the door for you to see new opportunities and begin to create new outcomes in your life.

Chapter 4:

Identifying The Outcome

"...and just when the caterpillar thought its life was coming to an end it became a butterfly."

-Kristen Jongen in Growing Wings

We've got good news and bad news for you.

The bad news is that, just like a caterpillar can no more prevent itself from becoming a butterfly, you can't go back to the way things were before your free fall. You can't change what has happened. You can't pretend things are as they were. They are not. They never will be again. So, if you're hoping this book will magically put your life back to how it was before free fall, you will be terribly disappointed.

But here's the sunshine on the horizon.

The *good* news is that you *can't* go back to the way things were before your freefall! You can't change what has happened. And in that, you *can* make things different and better than they ever were before.

We know you probably don't believe it at the moment, but being in free fall is like being given a blank canvas to create something entirely new.

Think back to the first day at a new job. You probably felt uneasy, uncertain, and missed the familiarity of your old work place. But, if you paid attention, you probably also felt excited, energetic and eager to do a great job.

At the end of the day, there was no going back to how things were. You couldn't go back to your old job. That realization might have been uncomfortable for you. But in your new position there were also new possibilities and a new future on the horizon.

The same is true with your life in free fall. This is why it's so important to recognize that you can't go back to how things were. It's why you must begin to identify new, positive outcomes in your life. It's time to look forward to something in the future.

Certainty and Uncertainty

For the most part, people naturally resist change. We like to know that there is some certainty in life. We want to know that when we wake up, the roof over our head will still be there. That the water in our shower will actually turn on. That today will be another day at work.

In one sense, this love of routine is great. It means we don't have to worry about the mundane things. We don't have to worry about which way to drive to work, because we always go the same way. There are certain things we've just grown to expect.

Unfortunately, we don't lose that sense of wanting routine once we're in free fall. All of a sudden, all we know is that the certainty is instantly gone. We're left wondering what to make of our lives and how we can possibly put the shattered pieces of it back together.

In reality, despite our desire for routine, everything in life is completely uncertain. So what does this mean for us? It means that our lives operate in the realm of uncertainty. And because of this, we can always create something new.

Identifying and creating new outcomes – new things to look forward to – are integral in your recovery process. They'll help you land from the free fall on your feet, instead of on your face.

How To Identify New Outcomes

When you're thrown into a free fall, it's hard to even think of identifying new outcomes and possibilities for your life. Usually, it's because we're so caught up in what we've lost that all we can see is what's lacking.

For most of us, what's missing is a connection – a connection with another person, a higher sense of purpose, meaning in life, a job that provides us security and direction, or even a feeling of intimacy or belonging.

We feel pain when we feel that the connection to any of these areas of our lives are lacking. The key is to make a conscious effort to find new connections that will provide you satisfaction, now that you're free falling.

One of the best ways to find new connections is by asking yourself powerful questions. By asking a better question, you can completely change your outlook, and in turn, your experience.

Questions To Ask Yourself To Identify New Outcomes

Where do I want to be in five years?

What immediate steps can I take to start moving in that direction?

What would my life look like if I went down this path or that path?

What are the things that I've always wanted to do but haven't had the chance to do?

What are the things I've always wanted to do but have been afraid of?

What have I most enjoyed at any given period of my life?

What are my strengths?

How can I use my strengths to help others?

How can I use this experience to help someone else?

What do I like to do that makes me really happy?

If I could live anywhere, where would it be?

Where do I want to go with my life?

What has given me the most happiness?

Asking powerful questions like these will put you on track to identifying new outcomes for your life. You might begin to see some things that you forgot you really enjoyed in your life. You might see a picture of your life that you'd actually forgotten about, or never thought was possible, until your world got turned upside down.

One very powerful question to ask yourself is, "What do I want once this is all over?" Be honest with yourself. Don't answer this question from a place of fear. Answer it as truthfully as you can.

Then look at your answer and ask, "Why do I want this?" Is it a certain feeling you're after? Perhaps it's a certain ideal or a certain event that you want to have happen. Begin to ask yourself the deeper questions of *why* you really want what you think you want. Once you understand this answer, you'll start to see what you're really after.

For example, if your husband left you and you believe that you want him back, ask yourself the real reason why. Is it to have the same relationship? Or is it that you want companionship and security? Is it that you want someone to provide for you and love you? What are the feelings that you're actually after? Are you wanting to feel passionate love again? Tenderness? Intimacy? Security?

Why do you want to feel that way?

Once you know the answers to these questions you can determine what outcome you are truly striving for.

10 Years From Now

One of the most powerful ways to identify new outcomes is to try this little exercise. Sit down and pretend that you're talking to yourself, but 10 years in the future.

What wisdom and insights would the 10-year-later version of you share? What would he or she tell you about what really matters in life? What would she tell you was important to focus on? What would he tell you to ignore? Would she tell you about how strong you were in getting through this experience? What would they tell you that would enable you to learn from it? And, finally, what would she or he tell you they loved about their life now (10 years in the future)?

This process can be one of the most powerful ways to put your life in perspective, to see that it's not really over, and that you do have a future to look forward to. Give yourself a few minutes to have this conversation. Then, write down the ideas and perspectives that came from it. You'll be amazed at the wisdom and insight that's already sitting inside of you – right now.

Don't brush this exercise off and just read through this. Take 5 minutes right now to answer those questions.

Strengthening The Outcome

Once you've identified new and exciting possibilities in your life, the next stage in the journey is to cement them into who you are. It's all too easy to have these new dreams get crushed by the reality of your current situation and that clamoring Monkey Mind. It's imperative that you take these new possibilities from ideas into reality and in the next chapter we show you how to do that.

Chapter 5:

Visualize The Outcome

"It is only with the heart that one can see rightly. What is essential is invisible to the eye."

– Antoine de St. Exupery, The Little Prince

Let's try something.

Imagine that you are on a sandy beach. It's a perfectly clear, blue-sky day. The temperature is perfect outside. Not too hot and not too cold, just perfect to be in your swimsuit. You can hear the waves crashing against the sand and kids giggling as they splash in the waves. You hear seagulls squawking and flying by overhead. There is a warm breeze that kisses your face, gently tossing your hair. You're sitting on the warm sand and can feel it creeping between your bare toes. You breathe in a deep breath and let it out with a big sigh. This moment is heaven. You're completely relaxed and haven't a care in the world.

Congratulations. You've just experienced visualization on a small scale.

Visualization is a powerful tool to start to turn the idea of an outcome into a reality.

Visualization is the story we tell ourselves, and the pictures we see when we endeavor to make a new plan for moving forward in our lives. It can be the roadmap to the next chapter in our life. It's similar to figuring out the road you might take to get to a friend's place.

Here's the catch though. If we don't actively and purposefully visualize, our minds will automatically do it for us. When we visualize on autopilot – without consciously directing it – we usually visualize negative outcomes. Passive visualization can create a vision based on our past experiences and feelings and all the baggage we carry around with those experiences as opposed to those experiences that we are actively trying to create to move us to landing on our feet.

Let's look at why visualization is so important in recovering from free fall.

Visualization and Recovery

Visualization is an extremely important part in the recovery process. Once you have uncovered new possibilities and potential outcomes for your life through controlling your negative self-talk and entering into hypnotic meditation, it's time to begin to translate it into reality. This is where visualization becomes so powerful.

Most people simply want something different to happen in their life. They want to lose weight. They want their old relationship back. They want to make six figures a year. They want to get out of debt. The problem is that all of these are simply wants. There's not a lot of power, drive or emotion behind them, because they feel outside of us. Instead, these desires simply create a longing within us and a sense of powerlessness.

When you visualize, you turn the idea into something that you can actually feel, sense, and almost touch. In doing so, you begin to make it real. Just like how you could hear the waves crashing against the surf and feel the sand through your toes without actually being at the beach, you can do the same when it comes to creating new outcomes in your life.

If you've been laid off from your job and have no money in your bank account, imagine what it will feel like to log onto the computer, go into your online banking account and see tens of thousands of dollars sitting in your account. Feel how good it feels to know that you can provide for your family. Feel the security of knowing you have enough to fulfill your needs and wants. Really feel what it will feel like to be able to be generous with those you love or those in need. See their smiling faces and hear the joy in their voice as they say thank you. Feel the goose-bumps that a moment like this gives you, and the sting in your eyes as you fight back tears of joy, knowing you've made a difference in a person's life. See yourself feeling the joy of giving and see yourself saying, "Thank you" and feeling gratitude for your many blessings.

In visualizing and engaging your senses, in feeling the emotions and physical and mental sensations that go along with the scene of your desires, you have just taken this wish for more money into something that has a place in your life. It's difficult to understand at first, but once you can see how it fits

68

into your life, once you can feel it and sense it and once you accept that it can be real, the likelihood that it becomes real increases exponentially. This is where the Faith Phenomenon kicks in.

Why Visualization Works

Visualization is powerful because it begins to write a new pathway within the network of our minds. It begins to create a new reality for us. And when we're in a free fall, we absolutely need something new and different to steer us forward in life.

Visualization is so powerful because the mind does not distinguish between what you see or do in your mind versus what you see or do in reality. This point of view was well articulated in the book *Psycho-Cybernetics* by Maxwell Maltz. If you haven't read it, we highly recommend you do.

In the book, Maltz describes several science experiments[5] where athletes visualized themselves shooting free throws in basketball over and over again. As they did this consistently, their proficiency in the game improved as if they were actually shooting the ball. The only difference was that they were shooting free throws in their mind first.

Athletes, musicians, and performers have long used visualization as their secret weapon in performing at a higher level. Olympic athletes are trained to visualize their performances over and over again in their minds, experiencing

---

[5] Maltz, Maxwell, *Psycho-Cybernetics* (New York: Pocket, 1960) 35.

each moment of the race or sport before it ever happens on the Olympic spotlight.

Pilots do the same thing in flight simulators – essentially a giant visualization console. They practice moves and procedures over and over in an artificial environment to solidify the moves in their brain before they ever try them out in the real world.

Thomas Edison had the idea of the light bulb in his mind long before it ever was created. This idea of the light bulb, and his continual visualization of it, led to discovering how to build it – even though he failed thousands of times before he figured it out.

The reason that visualization is so powerful has to do with something called neuroplasticity in the brain. Your brain is incredibly powerful. And when we talk about neuroplasticity we're talking about the brain's ability to rebuild itself and strengthen neurological pathways based on how much we think about a specific thing or feeling over and over again.

Think of it as growing bridges from one side of a canyon to the other, except it's happening in your brain. The more you fixate on something, good or bad, the more these bridges are made in your brain, making it that much easier and faster for your brain to think and feel the way you've trained it to feel. The brain does this for efficiency. To understand neuroplasticity better, watch this great video that Warren created:
http://youtu.be/T38pDA6f9X8

That's why when you have something bad happen to you at the beginning of the day it usually impacts the rest of your day. Maybe you spill coffee on your shirt right before you start your commute to work. You might start to think, "Oh great, is this how the day is going to start?" Then on the way to work you hit every stop light on the planet and start to think, "Are you kidding me?" Then there's an accident on the freeway and you start thinking, "I'm going to be so late for work! Why is everything going wrong this morning?" Then you get to work and your computer won't start or you completely mess up the presentation at the meeting. You might start to ask yourself, "Could this day get any worse?"

What you're doing all day long is strengthening your neural pathways to train yourself to look for and attract bad things all day long. So what ends up happening is all you can see are the bad things that happen that day, and it makes it much more likely for another bad thing to come along.

This ruminating happens all the time when you're in free fall. You replay the same situation over and over again, strengthening the neural pathway so it's easy for you to go to that place of fear, doubt, rejection, despair, and uncertainty.

But isn't it also true that there are some days where you perceive everything is going right? You hit all the green lights. Someone buys you coffee and takes you out to lunch. A random cheque shows up in the mail. You make love to your spouse. You get a promotion or bonus. Your day is just on fire.

The patterning is happening in your brain, only this time, you're strengthening those neural pathways and training them to remember and look for the good moments in life, when everything seems to be going your way. This positive patterning makes it that much easier to focus on the good when you look for good things in your life regularly.

The same is true when you focus, repeatedly and habitually, on the new outcomes and possibilities you envision for your life.

In order for visualization to work though, you must not only visualize from an intellectual point of view, but you must feel the emotions that coincide with that experience as well. If you see yourself winning a running race, you want to visualize the pride and excitement that goes along with the winning. Feel the tightness in your chest from the physical exertion, the heat of running, the sweat dripping down your forehead, and the euphoric feeling of successfully completing a challenging race with your friends and family cheering you through the finish line.

Allow yourself to become deeply emotionally attached to your desired outcome in a healthy manner. Let those emotions of jubilation, pride, success – whatever it is for you – be your motivating factor.

Thoughts From Warren:

> *What I have found in almost a decade of hypnosis and counseling is that the more connected an individual can become to their desired outcome, the easier it becomes for them to visualize, meditate on, and achieve their desired goal.*

The more complete the experience from a mental and emotional perspective, the more likely it is that it will materialize in your life.

Getting Started With Visualization

Visualization doesn't have to be as grand as inventing the light bulb. It can be much simpler. And when you're in free fall, simpler is better. Maybe you simply have the vision for how you want tomorrow to be. How you want to experience a few moments of joy and gratitude. How you want to laugh. How you want to put on your best clothes and feel good about yourself. Or it can be about how you want to feel or where you want to be next week, next month, or in three months from now.

Visualization can be done in several different ways. You can sit down and imagine the outcome in your mind – the more detail the better. Or if you have a hard time doing that, then another great way to visualize is to keep a journal and begin to write out what you want to see happen in your life.

Thoughts From Margot:

I recall one time in particular when I was having some trouble with my son. I was trying to cope with where he was and work towards a resolution. So, I started writing in my journal what I saw him doing years down the road and I told that story through my journal. I saw him captaining a sailboat with a lot of friends around him. I saw him in university, successful, feeling positive and happy about his life. I saw him feeling confident, secure and knowing he has a direction and purpose in his life. All things that were missing in his life at the time I wrote out my story in my journal. What's amazing is that years later, it all happened almost exactly as I wrote it in my journal.

If you're someone who has trouble imagining or writing, then drawing might also be a powerful visualization tool for you. Draw the experience or the outcome you desire.

Or if you're a terrible artist, but still want the experience of creating something, consider creating a storyboard (also called a dream board or visualization board). Cut out pictures from magazines of your dream life and put them on a board. Use them to help you visualize the new outcomes you want to create in your life.

Maybe it's pictures of happy couples, smiling, laughing, and traveling the world together, or of a beautiful family, a new car, or a great job. Whatever it is for you, creating a storyboard can be a very influential tool in beginning to experience your new life.

This act of creating something, whether it's writing a story, drawing a picture or creating a storyboard, will cement your commitment to seeing your desire come true. It will drive it even deeper in your heart and in your mind, strengthening the neural connections to those emotions, your faith in the outcome and, ultimately, the likelihood that your desire will materialize in reality.

If you'd like to be lead through a guided visualization exercise, we've created a free audio resource for you here to take you through the process.

http://itsthelandingthatcounts.com/

Chapter 6:

Begin To Take Action

"Do you want to know who you are? Don't ask. Act!

Action will delineate and define you."

– Thomas Jefferson

As much as we'd all like, we can't assume that life will unfold as we dream it will. We have to take charge. We have to take some semblance of control for the vision that we have for ourselves by taking action to create it. This is critically important when your life is in free fall.

As great as it would be to assume that just by setting new outcomes for our life and visualizing them that miraculously they will happen. Unfortunately, that's not the way things work. It requires us to move - to take action - in order to accomplish what it is that we hope for. Yet, taking action is oftentimes the opposite of what we want to do when we're in free fall.

It's easy to feel like every action we take has consequences, so we deliberately delay moving forward in fear of making the wrong decision. The problem with holding back is that in taking no action, we are actually making the decision to stay exactly where we are – and we can all agree that staying stuck in free fall is not very appealing.

There is a great story of a bird that was perched on a tree. For months the bird refused to leave his perch. The townspeople could see the bird was suffering but no matter what they did to entice the bird to fly it would not move. One day a wise woman approached the tree and before anyone could understand what the wise woman had done, the bird fluttered its wings and began to fly. The townspeople were astonished and asked the wise woman what she had done. The wise woman said nothing. Instead she lifted her hand in which she held the sawed off branch on which the bird had been perched. The wise woman explained, "To stop our fear of falling, we must let go and trust our inherent nature to fly".

At some point, like the bird in our story who had to let go of the branch to fly you will need to let go of your life before the crisis happened. You must have faith that your new desired outcomes will materialize. This faith is easier said than done, but it's essential to moving forward. If you insist on staying attached to the past you will wreck the present and the future. You'll just get more of the same.

Thoughts From Margot:

I can remember feeling crippled after my husband and I split up. I was so scared to move forward with my life. I feared that in letting go of what we had I would give up hope that we'd be able to fix things and get our old life back. So I stayed still. I stagnated and delayed making the difficult decisions I needed to make to move forward. I couldn't let go of what we had. I so wanted to get it back.

Everything started to change for me once I realized that I had to let it go because the past was gone. We could never go back to how things were because we were not the same. I realized that our future was both burdened and blessed by our past and that because of that the past could never be repeated.

In order to take control I started seeking outlets where I could see a direct relationship between what I did and how it made me feel. I dove into exercise. I started really focusing on myself and I enjoyed watching the immediate benefit that exercise had on making me physically and, more importantly, emotionally stronger.

Physical Activity

When you're in free fall, your mind can become completely consumed with your circumstances. It can feel impossible to get any relief from it. One of the best and most powerful ways to break the inertia is to be physically active.

Why is this?

Well, consistent physical activity has a few benefits. First, when you exercise and elevate your heart rate, your body releases endorphins. Endorphins are the happy hormone in your brain. When they're released, they create the feeling of happiness and elevate your sense of self-esteem.

They are known mood enhancers and one of the ways that they are released is when you exercise. Your body creates endorphins to combat pain. It nullifies lactic acid that's being produced in your muscles when you're working them.

This means that when you finish the activity, you actually feel better and happier about your life. There's a sense of accomplishment, like you did something. Bit by bit, that feeling of accomplishment re-builds your sense of self-esteem and self-worth. It helps you love yourself and increase your desire to reconnect with the world and those you love. Exercise is basically the most powerful anti-depressant we have.

Just think back to a time you finished a really challenging workout. Did you feel a sense of accomplishment afterwards? Chances are you probably did.

The second benefit is that it gives you a feeling of control in your life. When everything else appears to be falling apart, it's the simple things that we do that make us feel like we have control over our lives again. This sense of control will bring you peace, calm your fears, and help you feel happier about your life.

Thoughts From Margot:

> *Generally, when I'm exercising, I am so focused on what I'm doing that it empties my brain of the worries I've been marinating on. I remember diving head first into exercise after I lost my job, after my sister passed away, and after my husband and I split up. The exercise provided rare*

moments of relief when I stopped thinking about the pain. It became my priority in my day to make sure – no matter what – that I got a work out in. Sometimes all I could manage was a walk. Other times I pushed myself hard. Focusing on the actions I was taking during my workout was almost like meditating for me. It cleared my mind of all the Monkey Mind chatter and allowed me to find relief.

Finding Your Physical Activity

So how can you begin to create a habit of being physically active each day so you recover faster? And how do you do this when you feel lethargic and unmotivated about life?

First, think of a physical activity that you enjoy doing and that requires your focus. Maybe you love hiking, skiing, or running. Maybe it's swimming, cycling, or yoga. Whatever the activity, it's important to pick one that you actually enjoy, but at the same time will require effort and focus and which challenges you. The idea is to do an activity where your mind can't just run aimlessly. That's why sitting on the couch and watching TV isn't going to cut it.

Second, make doing that activity non-negotiable. You have to change it from being something you *feel* like you want to do to something that *no matter how you feel* you must do. It has to have the same value for you as eating and sleeping. Every day, no matter what, it has to get done.

How do you make it non-negotiable?

Hold yourself accountable as if you were holding a child accountable. Keep a diary for the number of times a week you intend to work out and what you plan on doing. We recommend daily exercise, but if that is not feasible, then at least three times a week. Keep a record and tick off each day you exercise. Post this record in a visible place so it reminds you of your accomplishments and makes you feel guilty if you miss any planned work outs.

Additionally, get a friend or family member to hold you accountable. Have them engage in an activity with you, or join a team or a club where you are part of a group that looks out for each other. Promise the group or your partner that you'll pay them an uncomfortable amount of money if you don't follow through on exercising every day. Whatever you do, be honest with yourself knowing that in doing so you are healing yourself.

Reconnection

Another powerful action you can take in your life is to reconnect with family and friends. Social connections are imperative to your happiness. Make a proactive effort to engage and connect with people.

You probably feel like connecting with people is the last thing you want to do. You'd probably rather retreat in your shell and hide away from the world. We totally get it. But we promise you'll get through the free fall much faster when you surround yourself with loving people and engage with the world again.

Now, why is this? Well, the crazy thing about free fall is that there is so much pain surrounding the disconnection from what we had before. This is true whether that pain comes from a lost connection with a spouse, the connection with purpose, coworkers, a job, or the lack of connection with a loved one who has unexpectedly passed.

There is a sadness that happens because we no longer know who we're going to do the things we loved with or how we're going to share and enjoy those activities again. Those activities could be sharing a cup of tea, skiing, bike riding, Friday night at the movies, or gossiping in the lunchroom at work. It feels like we lost our sense of belonging. It feels like we lose our social network that tells us we are okay, that we're not alone.

This is why it's so important to re-engage with friends and family - to keep them close and do things with them. Go to lunch. Take a walk together. Watch a movie with them. Grab a coffee. Talk openly about what you're feeling. Ask a friend to call you every day and check on you. Say hello to strangers. Compliment the barista and make him or her smile. Focus your attention on helping someone else through his or her problem. Whatever you do, seek to engage with as many people as you can.

Finding these moments of connection will begin to rebuild that sense of belonging. It will help you let go of the old connections that are no longer working for you or available for you, and help you cement the new vision of your life.

In every instance when I have been in free fall (whether it was after losing my job, the death of my sister or splitting up with my husband), when I opened my eyes and saw the love around me I was astounded. Strangers, friends and family reached out to say, "I love you". Sometimes they said it with words. Sometimes they said it with action (the gift of a book, the invitation to dinner, the squeeze of a hand). And sometimes they said it with their eyes. I remember one day being in a taxicab and reflecting quietly in the back seat about where my life was at and the taxi driver, whom I had never met before, in a kind voice and with soft, caring eyes said to me, "You are thinking heavy thoughts. I hope God blesses you and eases them." As Kristen Jongen said: "I honestly never knew such love existed in the world. Let alone for me!"

Share Your Desired Outcomes

A great way to take specific action on creating the new life that you envision for yourself is to share your desired outcomes with people you trust. Sit down with a best friend and tell them about what you want to create in your life going forward. Share with them how you're looking forward to finding a partner with the qualities that matter to you. Maybe you're excited about finding a job with a company that values you and you believe in. Tell them about the family you want to create. Tell them about the trip that you want to take to Europe, or wherever it may be.

Sharing your desired outcomes with another person is a simple action you can take that will help make it more real. It's the first step in bringing it to life. And right now, movement and momentum are going to be key for you.

However, please be kind to yourself. If you confide in someone and share your desired outcome and he or she knocks it down, DO NOT share with him or her again. Give people the chance to encourage and support your dreams, but don't let them suffocate it once you've shared it. There is no shortage of people who will want to hold you to your past and rain on your future.

That said there are also *plenty* of people in the world that will rally behind you and encourage you to go after your desired outcomes. Seek out these people. They are the ones that will be there for you when times are hard. Just make sure you keep them close.

The Power Of Taking Action

Thoughts From Warren:

> *I remember when I was in crisis mode after my mother had passed. I was at a point where I had to get myself employed again. For me, this simple action of seeking and securing a job went a long way in helping me move from free fall into recovery. I remember the action of going in, sitting down and having the job interview. I remember landing the job itself and then driving up and down the highway to my new job. I remember actually getting that nominal paycheck every two weeks and how it solidified in a lot of ways for me that I was now moving in another*

direction in my life. At the time, I didn't know if this would turn into a career or just a temporary position. It didn't matter. Those simple actions, in moving in another direction, cognitively opened the gate for me to begin to think about what other things were possible for me in my life.

It made me feel like I wasn't in that state of limbo anymore. That my life was actually beginning to have some momentum in moving in the direction that I wanted to move, rather than being the victim and taking what life was throwing at me.

When you begin to take action in your life, even if it's in tiny increments, you start to feel like you are controlling your destiny. You start to see that your circumstances do not have to control your situation. The key is to build momentum. Bit by bit, step-by-step, action-by-action, you start to take back the control in your life.

Chapter 7:

Overcoming Roadblocks

Imagine that there is a rubber band sitting in front of you on the table. It's completely relaxed – just sitting there. You pick it up and pinch the ends with both your hands and gently start to stretch it out.

At first, it's pretty easy to stretch it, but, as you stretch it farther and farther, pulling your arms further away from each other, the tension increases. It continues until things come to a decision point. You can either let go of the rubber band and watch it snap back into place (and probably smack your hand in the process – ouch!), or you can continue to pull harder until it breaks and finally releases the tension all together.

The recovery process is a lot like this. At some point after you've been proactively cultivating faith, meditating, visualizing and taking action to create your new life, you'll meet some substantial resistance. This resistance is what's called a "roadblock". And it's really a decision point. An opportunity to decide whether to snap back to the way things were (and usually hurt yourself in the process), or exert a little bit of extra strength and break the tension all together so the roadblock no longer exists (or is dramatically diminished).

Roadblocks seem to come up once you begin to stretch yourself outside of what was previously comfortable. It's that grey area of going from the known to the unknown – even if the unknown holds the potential for incredible good. The discomfort in getting there usually causes these roadblocks to flare up.

Types of Roadblocks

Roadblocks usually come in one of two forms: external or internal. Let's talk about the external roadblocks first as they're easiest to deal with.

External Roadblocks

An external roadblock would be something like a bad boss, who, no matter what you do, is all over your back. He micromanages you, criticizes your work, makes extreme demands on you, and makes you feel inadequate. This person is a barrier to you and your happiness. Whether that's career happiness or personal happiness, this person manifests themselves as a roadblock on your way to a fulfilling work life.

The same thing could happen with a friend or a family member. Maybe they're just a complete downer and suck the life out of you. Maybe, despite your most optimistic outlook, they insist on running worst-case scenarios about your life.

Then there are those people who surreptitiously bring you down. Maybe they complain about their circumstances all the time, or they are victims of their past or present circumstances.

Regardless of how these people manifest themselves, the reality is they are holding you back.

They're not productive in helping you move forward with your life. They're certainly not helping you find peace and prosperity. In fact, they constantly make it harder for you to get there.

Dealing with external roadblocks can be handled in one of two ways. The first option is to engage in a conversation with the person and come up with a solution to the problem together. After all, they might not be aware that they're causing so much trouble in your life. A simple, direct, honest conversation can be all that's needed.

If that doesn't work, then the second option is to change your environment so they're no longer in it, or you significantly reduce your exposure to them. That might mean finding a new job, or seeing that friend or family member only a few times a year. Either way, the external roadblock must be dealt with for the sake of your peace of mind and happiness.

Thoughts From Margot:

> *When my sister, Gabriella, was undergoing her chemo treatment and lost all of her hair it was hard for her to go out in public because she felt so vulnerable. After her diagnoses, she resisted allowing cancer to define her. But once she lost her hair it was as if there was a beacon that went out ahead of her and yelled out for everyone to see: "CANCER PATIENT APPROACHING". She felt that some*

people just treated her differently because she had been diagnosed with cancer. There was one neighbor in particular that used to drive her crazy with her condescending sympathy. Gabriella would leave a conversation with this neighbor usually feeling demoralized and defeated. From past experience she believed she could not change her neighbor's conduct by talking to her, so she did two things. First, she avoided engaging with this neighbor whenever she could. Secondly, if she could not avoid her neighbor she decided to change her perception of her neighbor's conduct. She decided to laugh at the discomfort that her shaved head caused her neighbor.

Internal Roadblocks

Internal mental roadblocks are much more challenging to deal with. They can run on autopilot if you're not careful. Think of it as Monkey Mind Strikes Back – the bad sequel to Monkey Mind.

With internal mental roadblocks, a destructive conversation in your head can come roaring back to life. You might hear yourself say things like, "I'm not good enough! I can't believe this happened to me. My life is ruined. No one will ever take me seriously. No one will ever love me. I'll never find a man or woman like that again. I'm too old, too fat, too open, too closed to find love."

These kinds of roadblocks are insidious, because they cause you to doubt the new outcomes that you've created for yourself and that you are pro-actively pursuing. They attack your new dreams, hopes, and aspirations from the foundation, which is why it's so important to become aware of these internal roadblocks.

Thoughts from Warren:

> *Internal roadblocks are one of the biggest hurdles in addiction and compulsive behavior recovery. I tend to see the largest amount of internal roadblocks are within women with eating disorders. Their self-image and their self-worth are significantly correlated.*
>
> *Although I see plenty of internal dialogue in other addictions, a women's self-image and internal dialogue seems to have a stronger grip than I often see in others. The Recovery In The Now program that I developed spends a lot of time addressing internal roadblocks.*

If you ever hear yourself saying something along the lines of, "Who do you think you are? What makes you think that you are going to be able to overcome this crisis?", then you know you have absolutely found an internal roadblock. But don't despair. This set back is common. Identifying it is the first step in minimizing and removing the roadblock.

Thoughts From Margot:

> *When I lost my job, I started moving in the right direction. I started getting incredible compliments from people and making progress on my next steps. And then I remember one day I just woke up and I said to myself, "Look, who do*

you think you are? Who do you think you are that you are going to be able to overcome losing your job just like that?"

I remembered that my dad had lost his job when I was a teenager. He was a professor of philosophy and spoke nine languages. He was an academic with multiple degrees. He was absolutely brilliant. My dad was far more intelligent than I was, or am, and I thought to myself, "He was never able to find a job again after the University lost its funding." I started to think to myself, "What makes you think that you're not just like him, what makes you think that you're better than him, that you're going to be able to succeed, when he couldn't?"

Then I started talking myself off the ledge. It took some time for me to distinguish the fact that I was different from my dad, that even though my dad was academically brilliant, he was somewhat socially inept. Our personalities, our strengths, and the timing in our lives were all different. So, being able to step back and look differently at myself and shift my paradigm helped me get over that roadblock.

One of the simplest ways to begin to overcome this internal roadblock is to invoke the Faith Phenomenon and repeat this simple mantra: I can overcome anything that comes my way.

Say it again.

I can overcome anything that comes my way.

Honestly, you can. There are a myriad of examples of people who have gone through free fall experiences far worse than you or we have, and they handled it with grace and strength. You are made of the same stuff that they are. You're no different. Believe it.

If you forgot how strong you are, then go read stories or books about people who have overcome the exact same experience that you've been through. Hop online and find forums or articles about people who have been through divorce and come out the other side of the storm. Find stories of people who have been fired from their jobs and gone on to find their dream job afterwards. Find stories of drug addicts who have destroyed their family lives and nearly killed themselves and have come back to start incredible foundations and transform thousands of other lives. Find stories of people who have lost a limb and become extraordinary athletes and motivators.

Thoughts from Margot:

> *When my sister was diagnosed with lung cancer she was given months to live. My uncle, himself a cancer survivor of twenty plus years told her to ignore the naysayers. He told her to read books about hope, stories of cancer survivors and messages from people who inspired her. She did just that. Not only did she become a beacon for other cancer survivors, but she lived for almost five years longer and better than anyone thought she would.*

Fuel your mind with stories of redemption and success. This will help strengthen your belief that you will get through your crisis. It will help you see that all the hard times will eventually relent and you'll be in the sunshine again.

Thoughts from Warren:

> *When I was battling through the darkest moments of anxiety, depression, and recovery, I consistently looked to those that either had more time in recovery than I did, or to those that had overcome far more than I had with their issues or challenges. I would get out of the 'poor me' mindset and put my mind in the right place to move a little bit forward.*

Terry Fox

Terrance Stanley Fox was born on July 28, 1958 in Winnipeg, Manitoba, Canada. His friends and family all called him Terry. He was an enthusiastic athlete who had a passion for basketball.

One day in November 1976, while Terry was driving home near Vancouver, he got distracted by bridge construction and ended up smashing into the back of a pickup truck, totaling his car. He walked away with a sore knee.

In December, he started to feel pain in his knee again, but ignored it until the pain got so bad in March 1977, that he went to the hospital to have it checked out. Terry was diagnosed with osteosarcoma, a form of cancer that usually starts near the knees. He was told that his leg would need to be amputated, and that he would need chemotherapy afterwards. They gave him a 50 percent chance of survival. He was given a prosthetic leg.

Just before his surgery, Fox read an article about Dick Traum. Traum was the first amputee to finish the New York City Marathon. Terry was so inspired by the article that he started a 14-month training program and started telling friends and family that he planned to run his first marathon.

Fox's secret plan though was to run all the way across Canada, to raise money for cancer research. He had been sorely disappointed with the amount of money that was being put towards cancer research, and decided to do something about it.

In August 1979, Terry contacted the Canadian Cancer Society, announcing his goal and asked for funding for the project. After getting their support, and the funding and support of several other companies (and a prosthetic running leg), Fox began his Marathon of Hope on April 12, 1980 near St. John's, Newfoundland, in gale force winds.

As he ran, he raised money and awareness for cancer research. He was met with challenge after challenge along the way but he persevered. Eventually however, he was unable to continue running when he made it to Thunder Bay, Ontario and had to be taken to the hospital. His cancer had spread to his lungs. He had run 143 days and 5,373 kilometers (3,339 miles). During that time he raised almost 2 million dollars for cancer research.

Eventually, Terry succumbed to cancer when it took his life on June 28, 1981. But he will never be forgotten for his mission, vision, and message he spread to the world. Because of him, hundreds of millions of dollars have been raised for cancer research and thousands of lives have been saved or extended.

Terry could have easily let his circumstances make him a victim, and wallow in how bad his life was. But he chose to use his free fall for good and to raise awareness for this disease in the hope that someday no one would have to face the experience he had faced.

He paved a path of hope for all of us. Whether or not we ever face cancer ourselves, stories like this can be just what we need to put our lives in context and give us the resolve to get through whatever free fall we find ourselves in.

"Extreme" Roadblocks

In psychology there is a term that is often used for your negative or critical mind. It's called left mind. It's that little nagging, negative voice inside your head. It's the one that goes to extremes and tells you things like, "I'll *never* find another job. I'll *never* be successful again. I'll *never* find true love. I'll be alone forever. I'll *never* overcome my addiction. I'm a loser."

The problem with extremes like "never" and "forever" is that they can dramatically distort the way your situation looks to you. But sometimes, instead of reeling the negative thinking in, it helps to push it to its most extreme just to see how absurd that sort of thinking really is and to put it in its true context.

Thoughts From Margot:

> *I can remember after I lost my job that I was so scared of never finding another job. My mind would run on and on and I would end up taking things to the extreme. My mind would say things like, "I'll never find another job. I'll never be successful again. I'll never gain the respect of my colleagues again."*

> *And I remember one day taking these statements to their logical conclusion and honestly asking myself, "Okay, what if I don't get another job? What if I never work again?"*

> *And it was funny, because I thought, "Well, what will happen? And I started thinking of the worst-case scenario. I'll lose all my money. I'll lose access to the people and networks I have developed over the years. I won't be able to do many of the things that I currently do. I might have to sell my house.*

> *But you know what? I remember thinking, "It's not that big of a deal. None of those things are what bring me peace or happiness. None of these things really matter in life. Fundamentally, I still am who I am. I still have people who love me no matter what I have, own, or do. So what if I lose all my money. That doesn't define me. I'll still be me. I'm still worthy of love. I'm still capable of giving*

love. And I have people who love me and who I love unconditionally and always will."

It put the free fall in context for me and made the whole thing much less frightening.

Give this exercise a shot. More often than not our minds run unchecked and cripple us with fear. But if you logically take the extremes out to their end result and honestly look at your worst-case scenario, you'll find there's much less to be scared of, and you're far more resilient than you believed.

"Well, At Least...

Have you ever been having a really rough day, where you wanted to vent and be understood, but instead, the reply you got was said, "Well, at least...".

Maybe your spouse just left you and your friend's response was, "Well, at least you found out now."

Or perhaps you learned that your mother or father had just been diagnosed with a terminal illness and you shared your fear and sadness with a colleague and his reply was: "Well, at least she lived a full life."

When people learned that a friend of Margot's couldn't have children (after having struggled for years to get pregnant), they often said things to her like, "Well, at least you've got the freedom to travel" or "At least you're not tied down with changing diapers and cleaning up all the time."

While well intentioned, what she wanted was empathy, not a diminution of the importance of the loss to her.

While there is truth in the "at least" statements that people are making, the problem is that statements like that minimize and dismiss the pain that we're feeling. It's that lack of empathy that makes us feel disconnected and can often create a roadblock when what we're wanting is support and comfort. Some days you just need someone to listen to you and tell you everything is going to be okay.

There are two ways of dealing with these "at least" statements. The first way of dealing with this situation is to find someone else to provide that empathy for you. Talk to a spouse, friend, family member, or loved one, and let them know that you need empathy and understanding right now. Don't be afraid to ask for it. Say, "Hey, I'm having a rough day and I need to talk. I'd love to get a few things off my chest and just be understood. I don't need advice. I just need you to reassure me that it's all going to be okay."

That request will open up the opportunity to get the support and connection you need when you're having a rough day.

The second way of dealing with this is to provide yourself with the empathy that you need. Sit down and really talk to yourself in a positive way. Go back to talking to yourself just like you would if you were speaking to a loved one. Give yourself a break. Speak gently and with love.

Then go back to visualizing and reaffirming your desired outcomes. Reconnect with that deep feeling of what you're trying to accomplish in your life. There are going to be times when roadblocks like these come up. That's okay. It's your commitment to continue to move forward, to land on your feet and take life in stride that truly counts.

Chapter 8:

Resisting The Retreat

Imagine you're hiking up the side of a steep mountain. The mountain rises dramatically before you. You're following a well-established trail when all of the sudden, the trail ends in a massive pile of scree. It looks like there had been a landslide that literally buried the trail.

Your goal is to get to the top of the peak, but now there's no trail leading you there. You begin to hike up the landslide of scree. Your footing is uncertain. The rocks are unstable, sliding out from under you as you walk over them. As you take one step upwards, it slides back on the screen field. This unstable ground forces you to exert twice the amount of effort as you would have if you were on a well-marked path. It's tiring, frustrating, and disheartening to travel this way. Yet, you have to keep on your toes and keep moving forward if you're going to reach the summit.

Moving from free fall to landing on your feet, striding towards peace, happiness, and prosperity, is a lot like climbing a scree slope on a mountain: You'll take one step backward for every two or three steps you take forward. And the challenge is being able to resist the desire to retreat when the going gets tough.

If you've never climbed up a scree slope, we can guarantee that it is a frustrating experience. It's one that makes you want to stop and say, "Forget this!" Your footing is all off. You feel like you're going to fall all the time. You never know what is going to move below you.

However, there is nothing as beautiful as putting in the work, getting to the top of the peak, and celebrating the elevated view on a perfect, bluebird day.

The same is true in your life. Overcoming your darkest moments of free fall – resisting the desire to retreat back to despair - will bring you to a place of freedom and happiness you didn't know was possible. It will feel like you're moving backwards, but when you look back, you'll see that, bit-by-bit, you're making steady progress.

In our program, *It's The Landing That Counts Master Class,* we focus a fair bit in this space and introduce you to the terror barrier and how it can influence and try to push you back from getting the growth you desire.

Hope vs. Positive Thinking

There's been a lot of chatter in the last few decades around the power of positive thinking. The popular theory is that if you think happy thoughts, then you'll experience more happiness in your life. And it's true, to a degree.

However, what often gets distorted in this conversation is that if you just look on the bright side of life everything will be okay. That's pretty superficial. That kind of positive thinking is often based on making the best of existing circumstances, or as an excuse not to take steps to change your circumstance. As a result, it's often used as a fluffy coping mechanism to make you feel better temporarily.

When you're in free fall, feeling better temporarily isn't enough. It won't carry you through the difficult moments when all you want to do is pull back and retreat. You need something stronger than just positive thinking and affirmations. You need a deeper sense of belief that things can and will get better.

Just like that mountain summit in the story we told you before, it's important to have a goal to focus on, and the belief that you can make it there. This belief is called hope. Hope is really about seeing beyond your existing circumstances and believing that you can reach that higher ground, despite the current situation.

So how do you garner hope when you hit roadblocks in your journey to recovery? The best way to do this is to reconnect with your desired outcomes and visualize them continually. Every time you do this you strengthen your belief that it's possible for you to reach your goal. As you build faith, momentum, and hope, it will propel you up the mountain of recovery, taking you one step closer to peace, happiness, and prosperity.

Here's a simple little exercise that you can use to reconnect with your resolve and strengthen the hope that you'll get to where you want to be.

Grab a pen and paper and write down the answers to the following questions. Go ahead, do it right now. Don't read on until you've done it. You do want to have a better life, right?

Okay, good. So, now that you've got a pen and paper, here are the questions:

When have I taken a leap of faith in my life to accomplish something (big or small)?

    - What did I learn and/or accomplish when I did that?

Who do I know in my life that has inspired me to take a leap of faith?

    - What is it about what they did that inspired me?

Think of a time when you were scared or too tired to do something – even something very small - but you did it anyway.

    - What was the outcome?

    - How did you feel afterwards?

So, what came up for you? Did you see how there have been times in your life already where you've taken two steps forward and one step back, but kept going? Are you feeling more inspired and hopeful?

Our hope is that the answer is, "YES!" You have already hiked up mental scree fields in your life before. Maybe they haven't been as big or steep, but you can do it again. You are powerful, committed, and strong enough to get up that mountainside and claim the peace and happiness you truly deserve in your life.

Keep the answers to these questions with you, so you can always remember what you overcame in the past. That will be like fuel to the fire of hope to keep you moving up the mountainside of your life.

Below is a poem called "Let Me Share In Your Strength" [6] from Margot's father, Dr. John Micallef, that is great reminder of hope when things get tough:

Let Me Share In Your Strength

Source of power,
When I'm so depleted that I can't continue,
Let me share in your strength.

Ocean of hope,
When I'm so discouraged that I cease to care,
Let me share in your strength.

Fountain of mercy,
When I'm so confused that I've lost heart,
Let me share in your strength.

---

[6] Micallef, John Dr. <u>Joy is My</u> Gift, 2007, c. Dr. John Micallef

Castle of resistance,
When I'm so exhausted that I want to quit,
Let me share in your strength.

Badge of valour,
When I'm so anxious that I want to succumb,
Let me share in your strength.

Shield of protection,
When I'm so vulnerable that I feel hopeless,
Let me share in your strength.

Mountain of patience,
When I'm so disappointed that I lose faith,
Let me share in your strength.

Pillar of support,
When I'm so distrustful that I feel lost,
Let me share in your strength.

Foundation of endurance,
When I'm so crushed that my life unravels,
Let me share in your strength.

Pledge of victory,
When I'm so disgraced that I retreat in shame,
Let me share in your strength.

Promise of perseverance,
When I'm so hurt that I become numb,
Let me share in your strength.

Leader of the brave,
When I'm so weak that I refuse to move on,
Let me share in your strength.

Consistent Goal Setting

One of the most powerful ways to resist retreating back to your old patterns is to be consistent about setting new goals. Goal setting isn't just a one-time thing. And goals don't have to be grand. They can be as simple as "I want to wake up feeling grateful tomorrow."

One of two things often happens when you're feeling resistance. Either you've taken your eye off of your goals, or you aren't pushing yourself to continue to achieve newer and bigger goals.

A great way to combat against this retreat and keep yourself on track is to do a weekly or monthly goal setting check in. Set aside 30-60 minutes on a Sunday afternoon to do this. Go ahead and put it in your calendar on your phone right now. Set it up as a recurring monthly appointment. It'll only take a second. Committing to this check-in is an important step in achieving your goals.

Okay, great. Now, during this session you will write down what you have achieved in terms of your goals and the progress you've made. Then you'll write down what you want or need to do and the timeframe within which to do it, to move even further forward so you don't stagnate. The idea here is to avoid letting our mind revert back to that passive state where we don't think about seeing growth on a regular basis. Being proactive with your goals will help you stay on track to achieving them and moving towards the new outcomes that you want to create in your life. It will also give you an opportunity to see the progress that you've made each week or month, which will help in your healing process.

It'll Be Okay

We want you to understand something, it's very important that you believe this. *It will be okay.* You will get through this. Even if you feel nothing but darkness right now, we want you to keep saying to yourself, "It will be okay. I'm going to be okay."

Thoughts from Margot:

> *Whether it was losing a job or splitting up with my husband, I remember the pain was so excruciating, I couldn't see a way through it. Everything reminded me of the job or the relationship. And it got to a point where I just had to stop and remind myself of this simple mantra, "It will be okay."*

The pain that you're feeling now will not last forever. Even if you don't want to believe it, stick to it. You will make it through this darkness.

"Hope begins in the dark, with stubborn hope. If you just show up and try to do the right thing, your dawn will come. You wait and watch and work. You don't give up."

– Anne Lamott

Chapter 9:

Gratitude

"Just an observation: it is impossible to be both grateful and depressed. Those with a grateful mindset tend to see the message in the mess. And even though life may knock them down, the grateful find reasons, if even small ones, to get up." – Steve Mariboli

You know what's great about kids?

They're either happy or sad. There is nothing in between. No fake smiles pretending to be happy at a family dinner, but really moping about the fact that sister didn't say, "Thank you" to you for bringing the salad. No. Kids are just one emotion at a time.

So, what does this have to do with gratitude?

Gratitude is a lot like becoming a kid again. It cuts through all the layers of emotions and lets us experience just one emotion: being grateful. Just like Steve Mariboli said in the quote above, "It's impossible to be both grateful and depressed." We can't be both.

Gratitude is one of the most powerful resources that we have available to tap into, and new research from the last 10 years is proving it.

Robert Emmons, Professor of Psychology at the University of California, Davis, is the world's leading expert on the science of gratitude. His research has found that one of the reasons that gratitude is so powerful is because it puts people in the position of participants instead of spectators in their lives.

Think about it. Most of us are spectators in our own lives. We react to things that pop up all day long. But when you're grateful, you take a degree of control for your feelings; you make a more conscious choice, and put yourself in a more solution-oriented state.

This isn't just fluffy talk. There is a physiological change that happens in this state of gratitude. Scientists at the Institute of Heartmath have found that your brain function actually becomes more balanced and supple and your heart starts to beat in a more harmonious rhythm, when you move from a negative mindset to one of gratitude and appreciation.

Emmons research also found that people who are grateful are much more stress resistant than those who aren't. His team found that people who have faced extreme adversity, trauma, or suffering, but have a grateful disposition, recover from the experience much more quickly.

Gratitude gives us relief from the feelings surrounding free fall. It is one of the most powerful states of mind and emotions that human beings have. No other state of mind can bring us into a place where we are more open to possibility. It's a state of mind where ego can't exist. And this is important when we are in free fall because our ego is insatiable. It just wants more and more. More money, more compliments, more attention, more power. Ego gets in the way of healing and landing well.

Gratitude, on the other hand, creates a space of being happy for what currently exists in our lives – for what we already have. Gratitude does not allow for negativity on any level.

Thoughts From Warren:

> *After a long period of looking back at all the trauma and issues that I'd experienced as a child and teenager, one of the things that I had to do was turn all of that negative baggage into something that was useful. When I looked back, I started to see that all these traumas I had experienced had created this really empathetic, creative person. Now I could see it in a brand new light. I could actually be grateful for what I'd learned working through my brother's suicide. I could actually be grateful for how my mother's alcoholism shaped me. I could actually be grateful for those things because it created this person that now had all these skill sets that could never have been created in any other way.*

Gratitude is like getting a 10,000 foot view of your life. When you're in the bottom of the canyon, you can't see what's around you. But when you hop in a plane and can rise above everything, all of a sudden the beauty of the peaks and valleys of life fall into proper perspective. They don't seem so intimidating – the peaks are not so high as to seem insurmountable and the valleys are not so low as to seem cavernous. This perspective helps because, instead of being in the trough of the valley and in the height of the peaks, you're now above them, looking down with fresh eyes.

Active vs. Passive Gratitude

There are two types of gratitude: active and passive gratitude.

Passive gratitude is about the feelings associated with being grateful. It's what happens when you see an amazing sunset and you suddenly think, "Wow, that is so beautiful. I'm so lucky to be alive. Isn't the world amazing?"

Passive gratitude usually is something that happens to you. You don't intentionally go out of your way to create it. It's just a feeling of being blessed that comes over you. This feeling is great when it happens. However, when you're moving from free fall to recovery, the times when this happens can be too infrequent.

That's where active gratitude comes in. Active gratitude is taking pro-active actions to stimulate the feelings of gratitude. It also ingrains the grateful mindset into our brains so that we access it more frequently and consciously.

So, let's look at some ways that you can actively practice gratitude every day to create a powerful, transformative habit in your life.

Give It Away

When you're in free fall, it's easy to get absorbed in your own life. Getting outside of yourself can be one of the best things to do to give yourself a break from your own troubles. One way to do this is to make a conscious habit of telling someone – every day – what you appreciate about them. This can be a friend, family member, spouse, child, coworker, or even your local barista or sandwich artist. Let them know why you enjoy their friendship, the things that you really appreciate about them, or why you're so grateful to have them in your life.

You'll be amazed how much they light up when you tell them this, and how good it will make you feel to give these compliments away to the other people in your life. It might be uncomfortable and a little awkward at first, but that's okay. We so rarely tell the people that matter to us why they're so important in our lives.

In fact, one of the top regrets of people on their deathbeds is that they didn't express their feelings to others. It takes so little time to do this and can bring so many amazing benefits to your relationship with them. Just think about how good you've felt when someone gave you an unexpected compliment. It feels great inside. So, don't be shy. Give gratitude away by actively telling others what you appreciate about them and why they matter to you. Do this every day.

Keep A Gratitude Journal

Another powerful way to practice active gratitude is by keeping a gratitude journal. At the end of every day, before you go to bed, jot down two or three things that you were grateful for that day. There is power in the act of physically writing down the things that you *already have* that you are grateful for.

Making it a habit will also train your mind to regularly focus on how you are moving forward in your life. That habit will make it easier to feel grateful and happy throughout the day. You'll be building new neural pathways that lead you to a place of appreciation instead of a place of negativity. And wouldn't you rather build strong mental bridges to feelings of happiness than to feelings of despair, fear, and doubt?

But what if you have one of those days when it seems like nothing could possibly go your way. Should you still give gratitude? Absolutely!

Even if it was one of the worst days you have ever had, it's still possible to find something simple to be grateful for. Give thanks for the fact that you're still breathing, that you have blood pumping through your veins, and that you're not buried six feet underground. No matter how bad your life may seem, there is always something to be truly, authentically grateful for.

I'm Alive[7]

Tell yourself

"I'm alive and I am blessed."

Discard the inventory you keep

Of the ways life has cheated you;

You're alive:

Act alive.

Keeping track of the small and big things that you appreciate in life will, over time, build up a library of great things that you either have in your life or that have happened to you. You can go back and read through your journal, looking at all the things you have or have experienced that are great in your life.

Thoughts From Margot:

I practice gratitude daily. I write in my gratitude journal – usually two or three things – listing experiences or people that I'm grateful for that day and that are different from what I'd written in previous days.

What I've found is that when I first started keeping my gratitude journal, the things I said I was grateful for were significant and macro in nature. Things like: my life, my son, my friends, my wealth, etc. However, the longer I kept

---

[7] Micallef, John Dr. Joy is My Gift, 2007, c. Dr. John Micallef

my gratitude journal, the more refined and detailed my entries became.

For example, I recently wrote in my journal that I was grateful for the beautiful weather and joy I felt skiing down a black diamond run in Aspen. I was grateful obviously because of the beauty of the outdoors, but I was also grateful because there was a time after my husband and I split up when I couldn't even have conceived that I'd be able to ski with such confidence.

The Little Things

Have you ever started shopping for a specific car? Maybe it was a Honda Element from a specific year. You probably started doing research on the car, reading reviews about it, perusing websites that tell you all about its features and benefits, and finding out as much information as you can about it. Maybe you went to a few car dealers and test drove it. You started focusing intently on getting that car.

And we bet something funny probably happened at that point. All of a sudden, you started noticing that car *everywhere* in your city. You started seeing it when you were out driving, walking to work, running errands, or out exercising. Before you decided you wanted to buy that car, you might have thought only a few people in town owned that model, but now you can't stop seeing it. It's pretty much everywhere, like the universe is teasing you to buy it.

Here's the funny thing. That model of car has always been abundant in your town. What changed was that you *started noticing them*. We'll say that again because it's so important. <u>You</u> *started noticing them*.

Thoughts From Warren:

> *The more attention we pay to change, the more change we get.*

The reason you started noticing them was because you began to fixate your attention on it. You thought about it, researched, read, studied, did everything you could to find out about and then acquire this car.

Well, the same thing is true when you pro-actively switch your mindset from a place of negativity to consistent gratitude. You start to see all sorts of good things showing up in your life, to the point where, it's as if you're surrounded by only good things. You can't help but see it all around you.

When you're in free fall, the opposite is true. You're fixated, focused, immersed in everything that has fallen apart in your life. As a result, you end up getting more negativity in your life because that's all you're looking for. When you start to look for something else, then all of a sudden you realize it's already all around you.

Pay attention to the little things that are going well in your life right now. Notice when someone gives you a smile, when a car stops for you to let you cross the street, when you get that first sip of warm coffee in the morning, that you woke up in a bed, the way the sun reflected off that building, or any number of beautiful little things that make life wonderful.

Bit by bit, just like seeing your new car everywhere, you'll start to see good things everywhere.

Thoughts from Warren:

> *In most cases in day-to-day life when it comes to gratitude, I often go with the "K.I.S." approach. Keep It Simple. I am a lover of nature so things as simple as trees, fresh air, flowers and the smile on my son's face is generally enough to keep perspective on what is important in life and keep my mood and mind in check.*

Thoughts from Margot:

> *The first thing I do when I wake up in the morning is say, "Thank you for the bed I'm sleeping on." Sometimes that bed might not be mine because I travel so much. It might be a friend's pull out sofa, my mum's single bed in her guest room, or a bed in a hotel room. But regardless of the size or location of the bed, I express my gratitude.*

Putting It In Perspective

Thoughts From Margot:

A few years ago my son and I were building a home in Mexico. We were doing it with the charitable organization called Youth With A Mission and their program was called Homes of Hope.

I remember we spent three days building a home in Mexico. It was a modest home for a family that had been identified as in need. The first time I decided to do this was because my son was a child of abundance. I was grateful that I had been able to provide for him in that fashion since my parents couldn't always provide for my siblings and me in the same way.

However, the result of my continued generosity towards my son was that he often learned to expect things, and being young (he was ten at the time), it was all about him wanting more.

My thinking was to show him the reality of how some people lived. So, we went down to Mexico with this intention. The funny thing though is that it soon stopped being about my son, or even about the family we were building the home for. It became about me. It was about feeding my soul and giving back.

The finished home was a little bit larger than a single room. It had no running water. There was a space where the family all slept and a space where the family ate. There were no other rooms. No privacy, no latrines, no place for them to wash.

I remember, at one point, the kids all got a little bored as we neared completion of the building, and we were working on the little nit-picky things that needed to get done. So, I said to my son, "Gather up all the other kids and go do something productive."

He gathered up all the kids – the kids from the ghetto where we were building and also our own kids that were there with us. They all started playing soccer. The soccer field was literally just a field of dirt. And there was a sewage stream running right through a trench next to it. The smell was terrible.

But all the kids were having a blast. It was such a contrast from the kind of things that our kids do in North America where they've got so much abundance.

After that, we went deeper into the ghetto where people were living in even worse conditions. People were living in makeshift tents and trying to find shelter. We brought blankets and food to give out. And the people were so eager for what we had to offer that they started grabbing at us and grabbing things out of our hands. And I remember crying uncontrollably.

We got back in the vans and went back to the hotel, but I couldn't stop crying. And my son, looked up at me with his ten year old eyes, and said, "Mom, what's wrong? Why are you crying? You know, we just built a home for someone."

And I said, "Yes, I know that, but we built one home for one family and I looked at all those other families that don't have homes. How are we going to help all of them? The people in that ghetto are just one little corner of one little part of this earth. There are so many more corners like that. How are we going to help all of those people?"

And he said to me, "Mom, we built a home for one family."

And in that moment, it sort of struck me that we have to be grateful for what we can do. - to be grateful for the little things. Even if we couldn't do the same for everybody else, we did one thing that was of significance to that family.

When we're in free fall it can be difficult to feel grateful. It's easy to lose perspective and be consumed by the pain, worry and shame of the crisis that we're in. We get it. It's completely understandable, but to overcome the crisis and land well, the victim mentality has to go.

Gratitude is the most powerful facilitator to shedding this victim cloak and taking control of your life. And as you consistently practice this consciousness of appreciation and put your life and your experience into perspective, you'll be ready for the landing.

Chapter 10:

The LANDING – Claiming Your New Life and Continuing The Journey

"No man ever steps in the same river twice, for it's not the same river and he's not the same man." – Heraclitus

It really is the landing that counts.

When you come out the other side, you will not be the same person. And that's a good thing.

In life, there will always be moments of free fall, always moments of uncertainty, always moments where you get knocked down. But it really isn't about whether or not you'll get knocked down. You will. It's a fact. The real question is, "How will you land?"

There is a great scene from the movie Rocky Balboa that really illustrates this concept. Whether or not you thought a movie about a 60-year-old boxer was a good idea, this illustration is a winning thought.

In the scene, Rocky is speaking to his son outside on the street. His son is arguing with him, embarrassed that his dad is going to box again at his age. He's tired of being under his father's shadow. Rocky looks at his son and says...

"Let me tell you something you already know. The world ain't all sunshine and rainbows. It's a very mean and nasty place, and I don't care how tough you are, it will beat you to your knees and keep you there permanently if you let it. You, me, or nobody is gonna hit as hard as life. But it ain't about how hard you hit. It's about how hard you can get hit and keep moving forward; how much you can take and keep moving forward. That's how winning is done! Now, if you know what you're worth, then go out and get what you're worth. But you gotta be willing to take the hits, and not pointing fingers saying you ain't where you wanna be because of him, or her, or anybody. Cowards do that and that ain't you. You're better than that!"

The landing is really a mindset. It's a place of recognition, where you can look back at the maelstrom and say to yourself, "I survived and I'm stronger for it. What's next in life?"

Recognizing Your Progress

It's not always immediately apparent that you've landed. It's kind of like growing a garden. It starts with a seed. And for a long time it seems like nothing is happening then all of a sudden there are tomatoes hanging off of that plant. Landing is very much an organic process. You might recognize it through a conversation you have with someone, or when you're quiet and reflecting, or when you're journaling.

Maybe you run into someone you haven't seen for a few months or years and they point out the dramatic change that your life has gone through, and all of a sudden, you think, "Yeah, I guess I have changed. Look how far I've come."

Thoughts From Margot:

> *After I lost my job, I worked very hard at trying to re-establish myself in business. I founded my company, Oliver Capital Partners, and through the company I invested in a radio broadcasting business. I provided consulting work to my former employer, and I got retainers from other significant companies. I was also hired as an adjunct professor at a prominent university in Canada to teach a course to MBA students. I was offered directorships on some significant public and quasi-public company boards. Honestly, I hadn't looked up. I just kept working. It wasn't until a friend pointed out to me all that I had going for me, that I realized, I had, in fact, landed.*

Another friend had a real estate development business with his father. As a result of their bank prematurely calling their loan, he and his father were put in a very vulnerable financial position. The two worked for years to try and shore themselves up by building a nest egg so that they were never vulnerable to any bank again. They worked ferociously, piling up money, but never stopped to count it.

Then, one day, a friend of theirs asked, "Why are you guys working so hard?"

When they explained they were trying to build a nest egg, their friend responded, "Well, have you ever stopped to count what you've piled up?"

When they took a look and counted it up, to their surprise, they had amassed a fortune worth tens of millions of dollars. They had landed!

If you don't stop and take the time to look, it can be hard to see that you have moved forward!

Thoughts From Warren:

> *I remember visiting the therapist I worked with during my breakdown months after I had gone back to work. It had been a fair bit of time since my last visit. He asked me several questions regarding what I was doing and how I was fairing.*

> *I focused on the depression I was still dealing with and was unable to see the massive progress I had made – how I had gone from being unable to work and crying many times a day, to working full time and becoming productive.*

> *At that moment my therapist made clear how much I had progressed. He pointed out the huge leaps I had made. I was functional where previously I had not been. I realized*

I had landed. It didn't mean that I was 100% out of the woods but – wow! - my life was different and much better!

A great way to intentionally prompt you to see the landing is to ask yourself a few powerful questions:

> *Where was I in my free fall one month ago? Six months ago? A year ago?*
>
> *Where was my life at each of those points?*
>
> *Where is my life currently?*
>
> *How have I changed or grown since then?*

What did you see that has changed as you reflect back? Are you less afraid than you were before? Do you have more moments of laughter? Are you sleeping better (even if it's only 5 minutes extra)? Have you been more active lately? Do you feel peaceful more often? Have you let some things go?

Take some time to think about all the big and small progress that you've made as you've moved through the free fall. And if you're having a hard time coming up with anything, then ask a close friend or family member if they notice any changes in you (even just the tiny changes). Believe us, they notice.

Make sure you write down in your gratitude journal the changes that you or your close ones noticed as you look back through your journey from free fall to landing. This will help cement the changes and give you even more hope for the future. Which brings us to the next important part in landing on your feet: Owning It.

Own It

Have you ever had someone give you a compliment, and then you brushed it off like it wasn't a big deal?

Maybe a coworker said something like, "That was so amazing how you handled that client. I wish I could have handled that problem like you did. Great job."

Your response was probably something like, "Oh, it's not a big deal. She wasn't really that challenging."

While modesty is great, there is an underlying issue. By rejecting a compliment, we deny our growth and don't acknowledge our landing - we don't allow ourselves to *own* our growth. And really, the compliment is just an acknowledgement of our growth and our movement forward out of free fall.

What if you were to actually *own* the compliments you received? What if you internally acknowledged them and used them to make you even better?

A simple "thank you" would suffice. And then you quietly just let the acknowledgment settle over you while you take ownership of it.

As you move from free fall to recovery you might grow impatient with your progress. You may feel as if things *should be happening faster.*

"Well, I should have let this go already."

"I should have gotten over him sooner."

"I should have found a new job by now."

"I should have broken my addiction by now."

"I should have found love by now."

"Everyone else is there, I should be there too."

All of these "shoulds" do us no good. As motivational speaker Tony Robbins says, "We *should* all over ourselves." When we do this we negate our growth.

What's more empowering is to take ownership of the experience and growth that has come from it. To acknowledge the suffering that we went through, but to value how it has made you stronger and more resilient than before.

From Margot:

I remember when my husband and I split up, walking away saying to myself, "I never imagined my life with him." But I had to recognize that our experiences are what they are and we can't pretend that they didn't happen. I couldn't pretend that I had had the perfect relationship, because nobody does. So instead of denying my experiences, I embraced them.

My husband taught me how to ski. I had never skied with anyone except him. He used to carry my skis and help me put my boots on. After we split up, I was determined not to lose the things that I enjoyed in life, just because I could no longer do them with him. So I started skiing by myself. I was completely outside of my comfort zone initially. And I cried a few times wondering what the heck I was doing. But eventually I got comfortable and the more I did this, the more comfortable I became with doing things alone and the stronger I felt. And the more comfortable and strong I became, the easier it was for me to see that I had landed.

Chapter 11:

Giving Back

"The best way to find yourself is to lose yourself in the service of others." –Mahatma Gandhi

Giving back to others who have struggled with the same experience is an important final step in your own transition from free fall to landing firmly on your feet. Giving back does three powerful things.

First, it solidifies the changes that you have made for yourself because you begin to help teach another how to get through it. Second, it holds you to a higher degree of accountability because now you are a role-model for someone else. And third, it gets you outside of yourself.

Many of the most effective addiction and recovery programs, like Warren's three month Recovery In The Now™ program, incorporate a major emphasis on giving back to solidify the transformation. Your journey from free fall to landing firmly on your feet is no different. Nothing will solidify your landing like giving back.

Recovery In The Now™ will teach you how to overcome addiction and solidify your change by giving back to others. Find out more here:

http://myrecoveryinthenow.com

Meaning To The Mess

When you've been through hell and back, it's easy to wonder, "Why did I have to go through this?"

There are only two reasonable answers to that question. The first, is so you personally could grow. Maybe there were lessons you needed to learn, or hardships that helped make you into an even stronger person, preparing you for future challenges and opportunities. As trite as it sounds, we only grow when things are difficult.

The second reason to go through the free fall is so you can help others grow through their own similar struggles. Every single one of us has had help from someone else who has been through a tough situation. Whether that was learning how to get hired for a job, how to ride a bike, or how to bounce back from bankruptcy, we grow faster when we learn from other people's experiences. In fact, that's what this book is about. We've been through our own free fall (more than once) and have made it out the other side. We want you to land as quickly as you can, so we're sharing what we've learned and giving back to you.

Giving back also helps give meaning to the mess that is inherently created in free fall. It lets you see how your own suffering has value to the degree that it helps alleviate others' suffering.

Make no mistake, God, the Universe, whatever you want to call it, uses our most difficult moments as springboards for our greatest moments of triumph and growth.

Being A Light For Others

Human beings are funny. We get wrapped up in our lives and become self-absorbed with our problems, our goals, and our frustrations. Just try to change lanes on the freeway at rush hour in a big city like Toronto or Los Angeles. You'll see how self-absorbed people can be. There will be lots of resistance when you try and "sneak" into their lane!

The problem with being self-absorbed is that you only get one perspective: your own. You can't see anything else.

Giving back and helping others pulls you outside of your own bubble and lets you see a different view. And there is nothing more powerful than moving out of those feelings of anxiety and depression that you experience in free fall than focusing on someone else's problems.

Thoughts From Warren:

> *One of the first times I experienced this feeling of moving out of my own problems was when I joined the volunteer fire department. I was regularly on call to help people in need. Every time I went on call, I forgot about myself. I was more concerned with the people that were in immediate need, the people who had just lost their home to a fire. This simple act of volunteering began to give huge amounts of meaning and purpose to my life. It gave me the fuel to achieve more in my personal and spiritual life because I saw how good it felt to be of service.*

> *I also took a job as a youth worker. I worked with foster and displaced children. As someone who had a difficult childhood, this was a powerful way to give meaning and purpose to those challenging years in my childhood. I could be there to help other children in need.*

How To Give Back

Every day you are surrounded by people in need. If you've learned anything from this book it's that you're not alone in the struggles that you're going through. People want to know that someone else has experienced what they've been through and made it out the other side.

One of the easiest ways for you to start giving back is to pay attention to the friends, family, coworkers, and other people that you come in contact with on a daily or weekly basis. Ask the employee at the front counter how they're doing. Pay attention to your coworkers' moods. Give your brother, sister, or parents a call to check in. Find opportunities to help them out through what you've learned.

Another great way to give back is to volunteer. There are countless amazing organizations that help people through similar free fall experiences that you might have been through. Whether that is alcohol or drug abuse clinics, Unemployed meet up groups, a support group for divorced men or women, there are opportunities all around you to give back and give meaning to your experience.

Take 15-20 minutes and do some searching on the Internet. Find organizations, associations, activities, or charities you might be able to volunteer for within your community. Identify the organizations that you resonate the most with and reach out to them or attend one of their meetings.

Another powerful, and potentially less formalized, way to give back is to be a mentor for someone. You can be a guide for someone else going through a similar experience.

Thoughts From Margot:

> *Whether through formal or informal mentorship, I work a lot with helping women in business. A big reason I do this is because, I can remember how it was when I lost my job. I met with a gentleman in Calgary named Dick, who I had been referred to through a friend. When we met, I told him what my vision was and my plan, and what I wanted to do. I was interested in advising on mergers and*

acquisitions much like an investment banker does. He was a successful venture capitalist with a 20 year track record.

His response was, "Come down to my office. I've got office space you can work out of."

I replied, "No, no, I think I need to join a firm. I think I need to work with an investment bank, an accounting firm, or a law firm."

He said, "No, you don't. You're confident. You can do this on your own."

Ironically, he had more confidence in me after having met me for that one afternoon that I had in myself.

So I went down to his office and he provided me with an office and an assistant for free. When I thanked him his reply was, "People helped me when I was young, why wouldn't I help you?"

And he kept helping me. I remember in July, only a few months after I moved into his offices he stopped by to check on me. And he asked me, "How is it going?"

I replied, "Fine but I'm worried about..."

Before I could finish my sentence he interrupted me and said, "It's too soon to worry. Worry in September." And then he would come back and coincidentally it would be September and he'd say, "How's it going?"

And I'd say, "Fine, except that I'm worried about..."

And he'd say, "No, no, it's too soon to worry. Worry in January."

And he kept checking in on me periodically and telling me to postpone my worrying until finally I stopped worrying because my business was a success. It was phenomenal. He helped me get through so many early hurdles and potential roadblocks. He was a great mentor. I show my gratitude for what he did for me by helping others. I try and do the same for other women in business. It's one of the ways I love giving back.

There are so many people that are looking for a mentor, for someone to guide them through their challenges and believe in them. As you progress through your own journey from free fall to landing, make sure you give back. Be a mentor for someone. Help them through the experience. We would be surprised if you told us you haven't received assistance from anyone. It may be that you aren't aware of it. But even if you haven't yet, you'll certainly have help along the way. So pay it forward.

Chapter 12:

It's The Landing That Counts

Thoughts From Margot:

The title of this book, <u>It's The Landing That Counts</u>*, actually arose from a conversation a friend of mine had with a former co-worker several months after I had lost my job. When this co-worker asked her how I was doing, she replied, "Are you kidding? Margot's landed in high heels."*

That visual of free falling and landing in high heels always stuck with me. I can remember sitting back and thinking, "Yeah, I have landed and I've landed well."

I now have a feeling of satisfaction all around me, that I've gotten through my free fall, that I'm better than I was and I'm stronger than I was. I have that feeling that I can do anything, and that if something befalls me, I can rise up again.

The same is true with you. You might not have landed yet, but we can assure you that it will come. We are all in a constant state of movement. Life isn't easy, and there will always be challenges that confront us – over and over again. Sometimes it's the same challenge. Sometimes it will be different. Sometimes it's harder to overcome than other times.

But as long as you continue to believe that you are going to land. As long as you use the tools you've learned in this book to enable you to land well, then it makes life that much richer.

"Bad things do happen; how I respond to them defines my character and the quality of my life. I can choose to sit in perpetual sadness, immobilized by the gravity of my loss, or I can choose to rise from the pain and treasure the most precious gift I have – life itself."

— Walter Anderson

In this book you've learned how to move from free fall to landing gracefully on your feet. You learned about the Faith Phenomenon. You learned how to recognize your internal dialogue and quiet the Monkey Mind chatter so you can take control of your thoughts.

You learned the power of hypnotic meditation. You saw how you can use it in your own life to shift your mindset and create a space for new possibilities to emerge in your life. Then you consciously chose to create and identify new outcomes in your life that you could rally behind and get excited about. There is tremendous power in finding hope when things are looking bleak in life.

After that, you saw how you can actively visualize your new desired outcomes, strengthening the emotions surrounding them and inspiring new levels of drive and motivation to create them.

Then you learned to take action to implement the new changes in your life - whether that action is through exercise, stress relief, reconnecting with friends and family, or taking specific actions towards your new desired outcomes.

You also learned that somewhere along the way you are going to face resistance – that roadblocks will certainly come up. But instead of backing down, you learned that these roadblocks are to be expected, and you learned how you can overcome them while still moving forward.

Some roadblocks are bigger than others, and at times you will get knocked down. It can feel like you got run over again. But you learned how to pick yourself up when you fall again, and to resist the desire to retreat back to old habits.

One of the best ways to overcome resistance and keep moving forward is by practicing daily active gratitude – whether you feel like it or not. These little moments of appreciation will compel you forward on your journey to landing on your feet.

And eventually, you'll become aware of your own landing. You'll be able to see the changes that have happened and be able to claim your new life. You'll be able to look back at what happened and re-take ownership of your life – putting you squarely back in the driver's seat and in control.

And finally, you learned how to cement your own landing from free fall by giving back to others in need. You can be a light for other people who have gone through similar experiences, and help them find their own landing, In doing so, you will not only change their lives, but you will truly change yours. You will have turned your own challenges into a gift to help ease someone else's suffering.

We want you to know that it has been an honor and a privilege sharing this journey with you. We hope that you will refer to this book over and over as you progress through your journey from free fall to landing, and that you always remember that it's the landing that counts.

We also want you to know that we don't take lightly the time you have invested in reading this book and investing in yourself. Time is something that none of us can ever get back, and we want you to know how much we truly value your time spent with us.

Now that you have an idea of where to go and what to do to stop the free fall, it is time to put into action the steps that will transform your life. To help you in this journey, we've created a 7-day FROM FREE FALL TO FREEDOM online course to help you implement these changes in your life. To get access to the complimentary FROM FREE FALL TO FREEDOM course, go to:

http://itsthelandingthatcounts.com

And remember that everyone suffers adversity. All that matters is how you land. You cannot grow or learn from stagnation. You cannot test your mettle without pain. You cannot forge new paths unless you are willing to veer off course. While it doesn't feel like it while you are in a free fall, once you land you will come to realize that you are the better for it – whatever path you choose to take thereafter.

This quote from Kristen Jongen from her book Growing Wings (2006) says it all:

Most profound was discovering that the anchor She had been clinging to so tightly also yielded the rope that bound her feet to the floor. In what appeared to be a desperate loss of security ... the cord was cut revealing her defining truth. She had wings ... and was always intended to fly.

You are capable of so much more than you ever thought possible. Do not be afraid of falling, because it's the landing that counts.

Your Free Gifts

As a way of saying thank you for purchasing this book, we're offering our FROM FREEFALL TO FREEDOM 7-day mini-course for FREE, to help you start taking back control of your life immediately. Additionally, we've also included a bonus audio meditation series to help you move towards peace, happiness and prosperity.

These bonuses are valued at over $297 and are our way of saying, "Thank You" for investing in the book and in transforming your life.

To get exclusive access to these bonuses, head over to:

http://itsthelandingthatcounts.com

Thank You

We never achieve anything alone. I have many people who must be thanked.

Thank you to my girlfriends Wendy, Willa, Arlene, Marina, Jackie, Laureen and Dena. Your love at various points in my life when I needed you most gave me the strength and wherewithal to find my way out of my free falls. Thank you to my trainers Eric and Yvan. You taught me the connection between spirit, mind and body and as my body became stronger so too did my spirit. And to Nick ... you arrived on an angel's wings and stayed for as long as I needed you. Thank you.

Thank you to my siblings who magically appear, in person, by phone or in spirit when I cannot see my way forward. My brother Joe who always reminds me that my "big bro" is there for me; my brother Rico whose efforts at being authentic inspire the same in me and my little sister Bun, who is always in my heart. And especially thank you to my brother Vince. You are never far from me and when I need you most I merely need to reach out and you take my hand.

I did not know there was so much love in the world, let alone for me. Thank you all for showing me how love can expand to edge out pain.

ILY

I also need to thank my co-author Warren, who provided the impetus to put pen to paper and hold me to the task at hand when distractions conspired to draw me away. I don't believe this book would have been written but for your tenacity.

Thank you also to Joshua, our editor, coach, wordsmith, mentor and friend, without whom we would have remained neophyte authors struggling to move forward.

And finally thank you to my colleagues Jinger and Natalia who manage to keep my office moving forward while I dabble in so many other things.

There is no question in my mind I would not have been able to write this book without all of you.

Margot Micallef

_____

I want to thank my wonderful wife Karen and my loving son Dylan, their support is what allows me to create and be of service to others. I must also thank my co-author Margot, together we have created what I see as something really unique and of great service to others. I look forward to our future collaborations.

Warren Broad

About The Authors

Margot Micallef:

Margot M. Micallef, Q.C. is the President of Oliver Capital Partners, a company she founded in 2003 to invest in private companies looking for expansion capital or an outright sale. Since its inception Oliver Capital Partners has directly and indirectly invested in a number of diverse businesses including: broadcasting, publishing, food manufacturing and real estate and manages the franchise development rights for a number of well-known quick service restaurant brands including Subway and Taco del Mar. Under Margot's leadership Oliver has returned up to 400% to investors.

Margot lives in Calgary, Alberta and is the proud mother of Christopher (who is now also her business partner). She enjoys the outdoors, including skiing, cycling, running and horse-back riding at her beloved ranch in British Columbia. Margot has been the recipient of a number of prestigious awards and was named by the Women's Executive Network as one of Canada's 100 most powerful women in 2011.

You can connect with her on Twitter at @margotmicallef.

Warren Broad:

Warren Broad is a clinical Hypnotherapist, life coach, and addictions specialist. Also a now retired fireman. Warren began his counseling career, as a group home worker, working with displaced youth and foster children. Warren's education is extensive, holding multiple diplomas in adult psychology, clinical hypnosis, an honors diploma in addictions counseling, and certified coach. Warren continues to add to his education annually. Warren is also the creator of the Recovery In The Now Program™ a coaching and support program for those suffering with addictions and compulsions. Warren has also co-authored the bestselling book "Living Without Limitations", and the "I am Anthology Love Wisdom and Guidance Through Soul Reflection" which continues to inspire others to break through their perceived limits and live the life they want.

Warren lives 2 hours north of Toronto, Ontario with his wife, son, and 3 rescued dogs. From there Warren runs his in person and online coaching and counseling practice. Warren is also often found on the tennis court, and volunteering in many local organizations. Warren's passion for helping individuals through their challenges is endless. Feel free to reach out and connect with Warren directly through his website http://www.warrenrbroad.com, or email at hello@warrenrbroad.com, or his Facebook following

https://www.facebook.com/pages/Online-Counsellorca

Made in the USA
Charleston, SC
13 June 2016